W9-BLS-668

NEW DIRECTIONS FOR HIGHER EDUCATION

Martin Kramer
EDITOR-IN-CHIEF

Moving Beyond the Gap Between Research and Practice in Higher Education

Adrianna Kezar
ERIC Clearinghouse on Higher Education

Peter Eckel
American Council on Education

EDITORS

Number 110, Summer 2000

JOSSEY-BASS
San Francisco

Moving Beyond the Gap Between Research and Practice in Higher
Education
Adrianna Kezar, Peter Eckel (eds.)
New Directions for Higher Education, no. 110
Volume XXVIII, Number 2
Martin Kramer, Editor-in-Chief

Microfilm copies of issues and articles are available in 16mm and 35mm,
as well as microfiche in 105mm, through University Microfilms Inc., 300
North Zeeb Road, Ann Arbor, Michigan 48106-1346.

ISSN 0271-0560   ISBN 0-7879-5434-9

NEW DIRECTIONS FOR HIGHER EDUCATION is part of The Jossey-Bass
Higher and Adult Education Series and is published quarterly by Jossey-
Bass Inc., 350 Sansome Street, San Francisco, California 94104-1342. Peri-
odicals postage paid at San Francisco, California, and at additional mailing
offices. Postmaster: Send address changes to New Directions for Student
Services, Jossey-Bass Inc., 350 Sansome Street, San Francisco, California
94104-1342.

SUBSCRIPTIONS cost $58.00 for individuals and $104.00 for institutions,
agencies, and libraries. See Ordering Information page at end of book.

EDITORIAL CORRESPONDENCE should be sent to the Editor-in-Chief, Martin Kramer, 2807 Shasta Road, Berkeley, California 94708-2011.

Cover photograph and random dot by Richard Blair/Color & Light
©1990.

Jossey-Bass Web address: www.josseybass.com

Printed in the United States of America on acid-free recycled paper con-
taining 100 percent recovered waste paper, of which at least 20 percent is
postcomsumer waste.

CONTENTS

EDITORS' NOTES

For the past hundred years, scholars and practitioners have carried on a dialogue about the appropriate balance between theory development and the practical application of the research. Different professional fields and disciplines struggle to define their purposes and their relationship to the fields they serve. These debates are even more pronounced within fields such as medicine, social work, and business, and within disciplines such as public policy (McInnes, Morris, and Carleton, 1982). The concern over pragmatism in academe has increased as public skepticism of higher education's cost and the demand for accountability have grown, which have been accompanied by a lack of interest in funding pure research (Fairweather, 1996). Several national commissions have formed to address the future of research and its direct application. One notable group from education is the Panel for Improving Educational Research of the American Association of Education Research, which formed following the paradoxical event of finding no nominees out of its more than thirteen thousand members for a research-to-practice award.

Within the field of higher education, research has changed significantly over the last century. From 1920 to the 1950s, the scant research was tied heavily to practice (Fife and Goodchild, 1991), as most faculty were strongly linked to administration or K–12 education. By the 1950s, the dialectic of theory versus praxis emerged, as researchers with disciplinary backgrounds and values began studying higher education. Since the 1960s, tension has existed between those who view higher education as an applied professional field and those who view it as a scholarly (and therefore distanced) discipline. Ever since, higher education has been in continuous flux, with perhaps insufficient dialogue about what constitutes appropriate and desirable research, with practitioners on one side and researchers on the other.

A number of higher education scholars and practitioners have voiced concern about the direction and relevance of higher education research. Patrick Terenzini, Lewis Mayhew, Clifton Conrad, Sheila Slaughter, and George Keller, to name a few, have expressed dismay with the methodological monism (Keller, 1998), its inward looking and parochial nature (Conrad, 1988), and the disconnection from practice and policy (Terenzini, 1996). Mayhew told the audience at a 1984 Association for the Study of Higher Education (ASHE) meeting that 98 percent of the articles and books in higher education are useful only to those who write them (Keller, 1985). The undercurrent of these critiques is that the gap between research and practice hinders higher education's advancement.

Not all agree. Birnbaum (2000) offers a different perspective by arguing that higher education policy would be "weakened rather than strengthened"

(p. 2) by creating closer ties between researchers and policymakers (practitioners). He suggests that researchers and decision makers use different kinds of logic to understand their worlds and situations and that for each, there "ought to be distinct knowledge-producing activities whose insights may inform each other but are not dependent on each other" (p. 7). That said, researchers and practitioners rarely contribute to each other's understanding and instead operate on parallel tracks, missing key opportunities to capitalize on each other's insights, diverse perspectives, and different ways of knowing.

The editors and authors of this volume believe that a primary factor impeding the advancement of higher education is that the research-practice gap remains fairly unexplored, and few suggestions exist to advance our thinking beyond blaming one side or the other. The small number of books, articles, and monographs provide only initial understanding. They usually argue for legitimating practitioner knowledge, as does Jarvis (1999), who calls for academe to consider a new type of knowledge that evolves from the practitioner-researcher. Other commentators suggest that some kind of showdown (between practitioner and researcher knowledge) is imminent, reminiscent of that which occurred when qualitative research could no longer be ignored (Anderson and Herr, 1999). Some of these same authors challenge the language of *war* and *gap*, suggesting that the concept of productive alliances will move us in more fruitful directions.

These commentaries fall short because each publication tends to offer a single position on a complicated issue. Without dialogue between researchers and practitioners, misperceptions are advanced and the gap perpetuates, with each side blaming the other. It is the assumption of the editors, based in part on their experiences in two action research projects that involved both researchers and practitioners, that both groups need to engage in a conversation to advance thinking about the research-to-practice gap, find common ground, and offer new solutions. The purpose of this issue of *New Directions for Higher Education* is to create a forum for researchers and practitioners to explore, reframe, and offer solutions to advance higher education thinking and application.

The intent is to provide diverse perspectives for understanding and moving beyond the research-practice gap and not simply to explore the issue. The editors invited an equal number of researchers and practitioners to comment and offer suggestions, including university administrators (including one president), association professionals, and higher education faculty and researchers. The editors themselves sit at the nexus of theory and practice. Adrianna Kezar serves in an administrative position as director of the Educational Resources Information Center (ERIC) Clearinghouse on Higher Education and has a half-time appointment as a faculty member at the George Washington University. Peter Eckel works at the American Council on Education on an institutional transformation project (the Kellogg Forum on Institutional Transformation) that brings together researchers and university administrators to understand the change process and translate it into learning that can be adapted and replicated by other institutions. Our perch on top of the research-practice fence situates us to move the conversation forward.

Over the past four years, Kezar has conducted research examining whether there is a gap between scholars' work and the research needs of practitioners. Her findings suggest that the gap reinforces a breakdown in communication and is perpetuated by perceptions and a narrow framing of the issues. Her study also suggests that *whose* knowledge is privileged in the researcher-practitioner relationship feeds bias, and she wonders if awareness of this hierarchical relationship is a starting point for moving beyond the gap. It is also important to note that this volume emerged from a symposium that Kezar organized at the 1998 ASHE annual meeting. She presented the results of the ERIC Clearinghouse study (Chapter One) and asked Marvin Peterson, Carol Colbeck, and George Keller to respond. The great degree of interest in the topic by session participants encouraged this volume.

Eckel's experience working with researchers and administrators around the issue of understanding institutional change points to expectations and perceptions of unmet needs on both sides as causes of the research-practice gap. At early Kellogg Forum meetings, researchers and administrators talked past one another, although all participants were interested in the same issue—better understanding of institutional change. Administrators believed that research had little to offer. As one pointedly said, "What can researchers teach me about leading my university?" The assumption was that the institution is in uncharted waters, that context matters, and that the questions change daily if not sooner, all of which are challenges not met by traditional research. Conversely, researchers questioned the idiosyncratic knowledge of administrators and perceived campus leaders as ignoring data and the conceptual work that might be helpful in finding solutions to the unknown. Each group could not understand why the other side did not see things their way. Participants came to appreciate that diverse ways of knowing could enlighten the unknown only after both groups found a common set of tasks to accomplish, moved beyond criticizing methods and ways of testing ideas, and stopped reflecting on differences. (They also grew tired of expending energy with little progress to show.)

To frame this volume, we developed the following questions from our own experiences and posed them to chapter authors:

• Is there a research-practice gap? If there is a gap, should there be one and what purpose might it serve?
• If a gap exists, how wide is it? Is there an optimal gap?
• What are the positive and negative impacts of the gap?
• Is it a phenomenon we should be worried about as researchers? As practitioners?

- What are the reasons for the gap?
- What can researchers and practitioners do to address it? Should practitioners be more involved in the research process? Should researchers be more involved in campus practice?
- How can research help create change on campus or within the higher education system?
- Will higher education research continue to take the same form? What new forms might emerge within the next century?

In addressing these questions, all of the authors started with the assumption that a gap between research and practice existed and that it was problematic. No one offered a counterargument (see Birnbaum, 2000). At the same time, none of the authors tried to convert one group to the other's approach. They started from the belief that the gap exists for numerous reasons, and it is time to move beyond the gap rather than to focus on the problems and point fingers.

Almost every chapter mentions Boyer's (1990) *Scholarship Reconsidered.* Perhaps more than any barrier, the notion of scholarship itself—what knowledge is—prevents us from moving away from this dichotomous relationship. Boyer calls for multiple forms of knowledge to be seen as rigorous and valid. Although he does not specifically address the issue of practitioner knowledge, his concept of knowledge as application and synthesis includes many of the ways that practitioners' knowledge takes form.

A central paradox inherent in the research-practice problem is captured in Chapter Six by Judith Ramaley, president of the University of Vermont, "The more that faculty in higher education programs seek status [within the academy], the more they are likely to pull away from contact with the real world from which they originally drew their questions and in which their findings might be tested in the context of practice. This seems especially paradoxical in the field of higher education because the object of the research in this discipline is the actual world of the institution that lies just beyond the researcher's office door."

This observation points to the driving forces of status and legitimacy, which are discussed in several other chapters. In Chapter Three, Carol Colbeck provides a lens for discerning the privileging of certain types of knowledge that are reinforced through the socialization and tenure process. Deborah Hirsch, in Chapter Eight, notes the hierarchical relationship of different types of knowledge, with practitioner knowledge on the bottom. Clifton Conrad and Ramona Gunter offer a solution in Chapter Four, but to get there higher education must move beyond privileging certain knowledge produced by certain people using certain methods. In other words, privileging "a type of knowledge" contributes to the dilemma explored in this volume. If rigorous knowledge generated by practitioners were appreciated on a par with rigorous knowledge generated by researchers, the gap might not exist. Perhaps the best way to think about the dilemma of the practice-research gap is to think beyond hierarchies and privilege, toward integration. Thus rather than focusing on the differences and shortcomings, on status and privilege, we might move beyond the confines of a dichotomous, hierarchical relationship. Although none of the authors suggests this action outright, their solutions and the future they propose make the case for it.

Some of the authors describe the possible rewards, benefits, and outcomes of moving beyond the gap. Conrad and Gunter note that knowledge tends to be incomplete because we examine issues from one perspective or by one audience. Ramaley describes how the complexity of problems engaged would be enlarged and answers to needed questions would emerge by moving beyond the gap. K. Patricia Cross suggests in Chapter Five that engaging practitioners is a professional responsibility, and Colbeck reminds us that many new higher education scholars have the desire to link with practitioners, which is why many education scholars went into an applied field.

Most chapter authors answer the question: What can researchers and practitioners do to address the gap? In Chapter Two, Marvin Peterson notes that individual faculty who understand the evolution of the field are positioned to determine the ways in which integration is important and how much change is needed. Colbeck argues that systemic change is necessary because ingrained structures (socialization and tenure, the peer review process) prevent progress. In particular, she notes that journal editors and review criteria need to be challenged, and campus and disciplinary reward structures need to be debated. She believes that listening and building relationships can break down the gap. Conrad and Gunter describe systemic changes that need to take place and present a new approach—interdisciplinary learning communities. They suggest that practitioners should be part of the peer review process to ensure that their voices are heard and valued within the community. Cross entices the reader with a new model—viewing the researcher-practitioner relationship like the teacher-student relationship—and notes the importance of accountability. She raises several key questions: What would the research process look like if we measured its impact on practice? In what ways would conferences, presentations, and speaking engagements take on new value?

Cross's notion of tying scholarship to active learning is further illustrated in the chapters on reading groups, think tanks, and efforts to expand institutional research functions. In Chapter Seven, Peter Eckel, Adrianna Kezar, and Devorah Lieberman highlight the work of campuses that have formed institutional reading groups in which practitioners engage with scholarship and reflect on the implications for decision making and policy. Hirsch describes the work of the New England Resource Center for Higher Education in bringing together practitioners from multiple campuses to read, reflect, and discuss to address complex issues. The think tank model represents an important opportunity for practitioners to teach scholars about issues that need to be addressed and to educate faculty about the swampy lowlands of practice (Schön, 1988). Ramaley sees the office of institutional research (which she renames the office of institutional studies) as a venue for providing synthesis and translation between theory and practice and sees room for both administrators and researchers in the process.

How would higher education be different if the preceding steps were taken? Peterson and Colbeck describe an uncertain future. Conrad and Gunter describe new interdisciplinary learning communities, with a values system based on Boyer's diverse models of scholarship. Cross envisions a system in which reward structures are modified so that illustrating the impact of your research on practice is a criterion for tenure. Eckel, Kezar, and Lieberman present a similar perspective, one in which the practitioner is learner, but the practitioners create structures to facilitate their own learning. Hirsch presents a vision of practitioners and researchers working more closely together to generate questions and answers. Her vision, along with Gunter and Conrad's, presents the most radical changes, as practitioners and researchers work together to define, conceptualize, and review research, ensuring that both voices are central. Finally, Madeleine F. Green provides a helpful synthesis of ideas presented by chapter authors, focusing on the way that national organizations can help in the role of translator and foster reflective practitioners. These different visions could be different futures or could be different phases in the path to breaking down the dichotomous relationship between research and practice and between researcher and subject.

Adrianna Kezar
Peter Eckel
Editors

References

Anderson, G. L., and Herr, K. "The New Paradigm Wars: Is There Room for Rigorous Practitioner Knowledge in Schools and Universities?" *Educational Researcher,* 1999, 28(5), 12–21.

Birnbaum, R. "Policy Scholars Are from Venus: Policy Makers Are from Mars." *Review of Higher Education,* 2000, 23(2), 119–132.

Boyer, E. L. *Scholarship Reconsidered: Priorities of the Professoriate.* Princeton, N.J.: Carnegie Foundation for the Advancement of Teaching, 1990.

Conrad, C. F. "Meditations on the Ideology of Inquiry in Higher Education: Exposition, Critique, and Conjecture." *Review of Higher Education,* 1988, 12(3), 199–220.

Fairweather, J. *Faculty Work and the Public Trust.* Needham Heights, Mass.: Allyn & Bacon, 1996.

Fife, J. D., and Goodchild, L. F. (eds.). *Administration as a Profession.* New Directions for Higher Education, no. 76. San Francisco: Jossey-Bass, 1991.

Jarvis, P. *The Practitioner-Researcher: Developing Theory from Practice.* San Francisco: Jossey-Bass, 1999.

Keller, G. "Trees Without Fruit: The Problem with Research About Higher Education." *Change,* 1985, 17(1), 7–10.

Keller, G. "Does Higher Education Research Need Revisions?" *Review of Higher Education,* 1998, 21(3), 267–278.

McInnes, J., Morris, A., and Carleton, W. J. "Theory, Models and Implementation in Financial Management." *Management Science,* 1982, 28(9), 957–978.

Schön, D. A. *Educating the Reflective Practitioner.* San Francisco, Jossey-Bass, 1988.

Terenzini, P. T. "Rediscovering Roots: Public Policy and Higher Education Research." *Review of Higher Education,* 1996, 20(1), 5–13.

ADRIANNA KEZAR *is assistant professor and director of the ERIC Clearinghouse on Higher Education at the George Washington University.*

PETER ECKEL *is project director, Kellogg Projects on Institutional Transformation, at the American Council on Education.*

A research study that examined the perspectives of practitioners and researchers on the current higher education research and literature revealed many areas of difference and some areas of agreement. This chapter explores the reasons why these two groups view the literature with such disparate perspectives. The findings suggest that both researchers and practitioners believe that the research needs to be made more relevant to practice.

Understanding the Research-to-Practice Gap: A National Study of Researchers' and Practitioners' Perspectives

Adrianna Kezar

As mentioned in the Editors' Notes, the field of higher education has been in constant reflection about its relationship with practice and the appropriate nature of research for the past hundred years. Keller (1998) lamented that the higher education research would scarcely be missed if it ended; he uses the metaphor of *trees without fruit,* suggesting that the higher education literature is filled with research, but very little is scholarship—that is, meaningful, important, or insightful. A common theme that runs through the critiques of higher education research is that there is a gap between research and practice.

Even if higher education research addressed the key issues in practice, many have suggested that there is not an open and willing audience for the research. Dressel and Mayhew (1974) noted that practitioners do not find it necessary to use research for decision making. They also cite the fact that students in higher education programs who study their own institutions often discover that their institutions are not interested in the results of the studies; they are not used to improve practice. The implication is that political concerns tend to override information.

A host of explanations have been offered for why the gap between practitioners and researchers exists. For researchers, tenure, promotion, and socialization processes encourage separation from practice; pure research and theoretical models tend to be rewarded. In addition, some research approaches tend to emphasize separation from practice as important for seeking truth and neutrality (empirical methods in particular). Interaction with practice is seen as "tainting" research. In the case of practitioners, their institutions require them to look at the immediate and urgent situations, which are often muddy and filled with interpersonal dynamics. The most prevalently offered explanation for the gap is that researchers and practitioners operate within different cultures, which develop separate languages, values, and priorities. There is no specific empirical evidence about what might be creating this divide within higher education (if it exists).

There is actually little, if any, empirical proof that such a gap exists. To provide evidence, a national study on the character (mostly the utility and relevance) of higher education literature was conducted. The overarching purpose of this focus group study was to examine whether a gap exists between researchers' and practitioners' ideas about what is considered significant and useful literature in terms of content, methodology, and format. Although the primary goal was not to determine why the gap exists, this issue was also examined in order to assist in developing solutions. Over 120 practitioners and researchers voiced their perspectives, providing a better understanding of the researcher-practitioner gap. Focus groups were conducted over three years at five of the major higher education conferences—the Association of American Colleges and Universities, the Association for the Study of Higher Education (ASHE), the American Educational Research Association, the American Association for Higher Education, and the Association for Institutional Research (AIR).

Research-to-Practice Gap

The focus group responses can be grouped into three categories—*shared perspectives, differing perspectives,* and *divergent perspectives.* First, practitioners and researchers agreed that there are few memorable pieces in the higher education literature, that they found more meaning in the literature outside higher education, and that dissemination of ideas is ineffective. Under the second theme, researchers' and practitioners' perspectives began to differ. For example, they found different content and formats useful and had different standards for assessing quality. Finally, practitioners' and researchers' viewpoints were the most divergent when discussing significant issues to study, gaps in the literature, future directions, and improving the higher education literature.

Shared Perspectives. This section highlights the areas of agreement between practitioners and researchers.

Memorable Works Missing. There was general agreement among researchers and practitioners that higher education literature is not as significant or useful as it could or should be. When we asked the members of each group to name the most memorable piece of writing in higher education that they had read in the last five years, ten years, and then without a time limit, both researchers and practitioners had difficulty noting a memorable work. Practitioners who did describe a memorable piece said that it shed light on or transformed their notions about practice. In essence, these pieces influenced the day-to-day lives of practitioners. Several publications and authors were brought up in almost every focus group—Boyer's books *Scholarship Reconsidered* or *College,* Palmer's books on holistic learning and community, Keller's work on planning and strategy, and Barr and Tagg's article on changing the teaching and learning paradigm. Practitioners in each group described how these works had changed the ways that universities and colleges function. Practitioners noted that most literature is not memorable because it does not reflect practice, nor does it provide insight or vision about practice. They were very interested in philosophical works that examine underlying assumptions. Works were memorable to them because they could see that institutions were transformed as a result.

Identifying a memorable work within the higher education literature was even more difficult for researchers. Their most common response was that they skimmed the higher education journals, such as the *Review of Higher Education* and the *Journal of Higher Education,* and the significant magazines, such as the *Chronicle of Higher Education, Change,* and *About Campus,* but that they hardly ever found anything worth reading. Researchers found the higher education literature even less relevant or helpful to their work than did practitioners. Often they were unable to provide a memorable work, but when they did, they noted either works that challenge current theoretical paradigms or ones that bridge theory and practice. The majority of the researchers saw works that are wholly conceptual or theoretical as the most memorable. One researcher said, "Influential literature is that which extends my current way of thinking, lens, or paradigm. Michael Coles's book on folk psychology challenged traditional notions, and that was memorable to me." However, many researchers also mentioned that significant literature ties theory to practice. Researchers described many of the same significant works that practitioners cited, including Boyer's books and Barr and Tagg's article. Though there is a slightly different orientation as to what is significant, with researchers leaning toward literature that builds theory in isolation of the implications to practice, there is the joint agreement that writing that brings practice and theory together is memorable and significant and should be more prevalent in the literature. The struggle to describe a significant work was troubling to researchers.

Finding Meaning Outside the Higher Education Literature. Practitioners and researchers were both likely to find the literature outside higher education more useful, but for different reasons. This comment typifies researchers' reasons for using literature outside higher education, "I read outside of higher education because the literature tends to be more conceptual and abstract and useful to my work." The second most prevalent comment was that researchers are borrowing heavily from other disciplines, such as management, economics, psychology, or sociology, because the theoretical insights are stronger within these disciplines. Another reason for drawing on other disciplines was that some subfields are not well represented in the higher education literature—in particular, organizational theory, teaching and learning, policy, and legal issues. The K–12 literature was often mentioned as a better source for information about subfields. Other reasons mentioned for reading outside higher education were that higher education literature is too specialized and narrow and that few pieces tie theory and practice. Some researchers found the literature *atheoretical,* and others found it too theoretical and removed from practice. There was no identifiable trend for certain groups (constructivists, women, people of color, individuals from nonuniversity environments) to express a particular belief. However, many researchers agreed that prescriptive literature, such as many Jossey-Bass books, is an overly simplistic approach to tying theory to practice.

Practitioners were more likely to read works from business and management, sociology, and K–12 literature. They found other professional literature or disciplinary literature to be philosophical, insightful, future oriented, focused on timely critical issues, and helpful to practice. Practitioners continually noted that the higher education literature is not visionary. This was the major concern and prompted the need to seek out other literature.

Differing Perspectives.   This section looks at those topics about which researchers and practitioners began to express dissimilar views.

What Is Useful Information?   When practitioners were prodded about what made them read outside the field of higher education and what would make higher education literature more useful, several themes emerged. They expressed concern that the higher education literature contains irrelevant topics (too old) and that timely and current issues are not represented; that it is too removed from the day-to-day activity of practitioners, with no bridge (practitioners were expected to make the leap), and that it is too theoretical and not sufficiently issue focused; that it contains minimal information about best practices and how to build practice and does not provide case scenarios; that it lacks the perspective to help reconceptualize frameworks; that it is too narrowly framed (looking at a phenomenon in isolation, which does not mirror reality); and that it lacks solutions or advice.

Practitioners perceive that academic publishing takes too long, and they think that the material is mostly irrelevant by the time it is published. Practitioners are seeking information from the World Wide Web, Listservs, and even newspapers that tend to be timely. Practitioners expressed concern that the higher education literature is too descriptive, does not include implications, and does not offer compelling details or nuances of situations. One person noted, "Too often the simple generalizations or principles offered just do not mirror the situations we face." In addition, practitioners are not averse to theory. In fact, they wish the literature in higher education were more theoretical and bolder in perspective. The problem is that theory is not made relevant to practice; there is no connection. Practitioners were quick to mention several nonacademic publications in higher education written by nonresearchers (for the most part) as the most helpful and useful to their work. *Change,* the *NTLF Newsletter,* the *American Association for Higher Education Bulletin,* the *New Directions* series, the *New York Times, Pew Policy Perspectives,* and *On the Horizon* were cited most often.

Researchers had a very different perspective about what constitutes useful literature. The most common theme was that useful literature pushes theoretical boundaries and perspectives or questions commonly held assumptions. This was different from the perspective that practitioners described—that literature should provide new perspectives for understanding problems. Words such as *controversial, pushing boundaries, engaging, questioning, critical,* and *raising questions* were mentioned again and again by researchers in describing useful literature. The emphasis was on raising questions rather than on providing answers. Researchers agreed that higher education literature tends to be written in somewhat difficult or "unuseful" ways. They thought that richer descriptions are necessary, but rather than describing the case scenarios that practitioners desired, researchers mentioned using fiction or stories, poetry, or magazine story formats. Researchers struggled against producing advocacy, perspective-taking, and solution-oriented literature, considering it to be problematic (they also perceived it to be the kind of literature that practitioners desire). As they saw it, researchers should not offer advice or solutions, and they believe that practitioners want oversimplified analysis of issues. Several researchers noted that they were aware that the literature they are producing is not as useful to practitioners as it could be. Those who do try to develop a bridge between theory and practice find themselves lost and seeking direction. Some researchers described struggling to keep in touch with the world outside the academy; they described themselves as separated. As one of them put it, "I read more of the popular literature so I can keep in touch with the way people outside the academy think about things, and this helps provide a bridge."

What Are Useful Formats? Researchers and practitioners differed in their notions of useful formats. The most common response of practitioners was that the literature needs to be short, concise, and summative. Readability could be increased by using bullet points and a common language; accessibility improved by placing documents on the Web. Practitioners desired a lengthy implications section and reference list. Literature that synthesized information was also seen as useful. Practitioners noted that if the writer has the audience in mind, the piece reads much more easily. They noted that it is apparent when the writer has not clearly identified the audience. The AIR newsletter was mentioned by many people as a model for information delivery. The newsletter is electronic, short, jargon free, uses bullet points, is audience specific, covers a range of important topics, and can be saved on the computer for future reference. *Change* was also mentioned as having a format that meets most of these criteria (with the exception of the electronic accessibility). Some practitioners noted that there are also differences in learning styles. Some practitioners have an auditory learning style, and as there are few tapes available on higher education topics, they call colleagues or buy audiotapes from other fields.

Researchers thought that useful formats are those that are unpredictable, varied, detailed, and have an emphasis on critiquing. Lengthy theory and methodology sections were favored. Researchers also noted that writing for multiple audiences is preferable. Theory speaks to various audiences and should be left in a more generalizable format, so that various groups can see the relationship of the issues to their work. Practitioners and researchers agreed that good writing and accessible language are key. Several researchers acknowledged their difficulty in producing accessible works and were working to change this. One researcher noted, "I read the *New Yorker* as well as fiction in general because it helps me in academic writing. I mean it helps me to write in a less academic way."

In some focus groups, practitioners and researchers debated the topic of useful formats. Several focus groups ended with a consensus that the literature needed is something between the bullet-point format that practitioners desire and the lengthy writings that researchers conventionally produce. There was agreement that neither format is very useful. The bullet points often oversimplify complex issues, and the lengthy articles are frequently a sign of poor, sloppy scholarship. There was acknowledgment on the part of practitioners that they need to develop strategies (for example, reading groups) for reading longer pieces because simply putting their hands up and saying, "I cannot read anything over six pages" will not help advance their thinking. In kind, researchers responded that they need to be aware that practitioners do not have the luxury of time to think and reflect that researchers' schedules (at some institutions) allow. Practitioners further acknowledged that they need to find the time to read research because it is part of their responsibility as professionals and should be a priority.

Defining Standards and Values: What Is Quality Literature? Given the responses to earlier questions about usefulness, significance, and direction for the higher education literature, it was not surprising that the two groups had different criteria for determining quality literature. Practitioners emphasized relevance to practice and the significance of the topic or issue studied as the top criteria for quality, followed by insightfulness or new ideas, good writing, and audience-specific writing. Practitioners and researchers were in agreement that methodology is overemphasized as a criterion of quality and that writing is important. Also, the emphasis on insights or breaking new ground was discussed by both groups. In general, practitioners focused on the research *product* to define quality, whereas researchers were more likely to focus on research *process* for determining quality. Researchers mentioned peer review toward the end of the manuscript review process (more reviewers means more timely reviews) for books, better-coordinated peer review, mentoring of junior faculty in the norms of the profession, and emphasis on good writing in graduate programs as keys to improving quality.

Conceptual strength and logic were the criteria most commonly mentioned by researchers; they were paired together in discussion. The significance of the topic or relevance to practice was an afterthought to researchers and mentioned only after discussed by practitioners.

Divergent Perspectives. This section explores the areas about which researchers and practitioners held the most disparate views.

What Are the Significant Issues? What Is Missing? What Are Future Directions? Unfortunately, the majority of the issues that practitioners thought were important are not being studied, such as assessment of distance learning, implementation of technology, international concerns, economic issues, institutional effectiveness, performance indicators, ethics, spirituality, collaboration between student affairs and academic affairs, the articulation of K–12 into higher education, quality standards, and relationships with the community. The lack of research on distance learning, in particular, was mentioned as a concern. One practitioner noted that she is extremely interested in performance indicators but that there is little mention in higher education literature. "I have to look to the business literature. I also find myself doing this to find literature on collaboration and assessment. I find myself in other literatures the majority of the time, and then I have to translate it into the university environment. But what other choice do I have?"

Another type of gap was the lack of studies on specific sectors in higher education, specifically private schools, community colleges, or single-population-serving institutions. Because higher education literature mirrors the research university's values and priorities, important issues for other sectors are often not examined. In particular, the largest sector—community colleges—tends to be mostly unstudied. Few people study higher education as an enterprise, from a macro systems perspective. Most research focuses on groups, programs, institutions, or state-level issues. There was also an interest in meta-analysis—research that accumulates many smaller studies, synthesizes the findings, and draws broader implications. Association reports (an example given was the Association of American Colleges and Universities work on diversity) sometimes fill this goal, but in no systematic way. A last gap was that the higher education literature is not visionary and simply describes the current state of the academy. One practitioner asked, "What will the university of the twenty-first century look like? Where are we going with distance learning? How is the enterprise changing? How might cost structures change? Is access changing? These are questions I worry about and cannot find answers to."

Researchers had few responses when asked about the important issues to study or the gaps in the literature. Although they actively participated in other parts of the focus group, they were mostly silent when these issues emerged. A few researchers mentioned assessment and learning outcomes as significant issues to study. In terms of gaps in the literature, they mentioned postmodern and interpretive theory as being lacking. When researchers mentioned gaps, they tended to think of them in terms of subfields (for example, organizational theory or cognitive science) rather than in terms of issues (for example, technology or learning). They might mention that there needs to be more research in the area of public policy rather than mentioning performance indicators specifically. Also, a few researchers mentioned that the way to address future issues is to apply new theoretical frameworks. One said, "In order to understand what the future college experience will be like, or how technology is impacting us, or different student expectations, or what it means to be a constructivist faculty member, we need postmodern theory for framing these issues and reexamining modernist assumptions that frame current thought and practice."

Literature gaps appear to be seen differently by these two groups. For practitioners, it is gaps in what we know about practice issues; for researchers, it is gaps in theory. The notion of important *issues* did not resonate with researchers. Perhaps they might have responded to a question about important *theories*.

How Can the Literature Be Improved? Although there is general agreement that the higher education literature lacks meaning and significance for the work of researchers or practitioners, there is not agreement on how improvement would occur. To understand the disparate responses from the two groups, one must understand their different views of what constitutes useful information and formats and what is important to study. Researchers thought that books on how to build theory would help provide the literature with a stronger theoretical base. Different formats such as poetry, fiction, or metaphor might broaden the way we express issues. These suggestions were developed from a perspective that the literature is not significant because it is theoretically weak and methodologically narrow. The interdisciplinary nature of the higher education literature was seen as both a strength and a weakness—the strength being that multiple perspectives are brought to bear on an issue, borrowing heavily from other disciplines; the weakness being that researchers appropriate a theory without careful review or understanding, leading to shoddy scholarship.

Practitioners conceptualize improvement in very different ways. They emphasized that the lens applied to the study of higher education needs to be modified. Researchers need to understand what the issues are in practice and begin to study these issues. Practitioners also noted that the values of the research university need to be examined and realigned to encompass the entire enterprise. The advice and solution-oriented literature that practitioners are seeking could be provided by examining the models in business literature or social work. Practitioners' suggestions to produce more visionary work and case scenarios may be addressed by some of the methodological and theoretical changes proposed by researchers. Thus there is some agreement about the changes that might be made to produce a literature base that is significant and useful.

Beyond the Research-to-Practice Gap

The results of the study clearly illustrate a difference or gap between researchers' and practitioners' views of higher education literature. Both groups agree that the literature is not memorable, insightful, or a source of important information. Therefore there is a problem that needs to be addressed. Higher education research still appears to be trees without fruit. What insights were gathered about the reason for the gap? How might this study move us beyond the gap?

The results of this study illustrate that the researchers and practitioners have different criteria for what makes literature significant. Practitioners and researchers use different language and see information in distinct ways. This *role* explanation tells us that researchers are producing literature based on their own culture and its rewards. The practitioners' assumptions and habits of mind are generally not taken into account; thus the gap exists. Nevertheless there were many points of agreement between practitioners and researchers. Researchers did in many cases realize that relevance to practice and some sense of direction or determinacy are important. There were some lively debates about the need for practitioners to assess critically the assumptions undergirding practice and to be more conceptual and for researchers to grapple more with the implications of their research. But not enough discussion took place for either party to believe that there was truly a meeting of the minds or new understanding.

Another explanation is that higher education calls itself a field of study, but there is no clear consensus as to whether it is a professional field or a discipline. In fact, this distinction has been debated in ASHE meetings and committees for the last twenty to thirty years. This situation may contribute to the fact that practitioners are less well served by the research, and researchers are unsure how much they should care. Comments from researchers illustrate this lack of clarity. During one focus group, a researcher was describing the importance of the research and literature being tied to practice. Another researcher contradicted by saying that the purpose of research is to provoke thought and build a foundation of knowledge. These types of debate were commonplace in the focus groups. How can practitioners understand what higher education research offers if the field is unsure?

There is a significant amount of research that indicates the influence of socialization and reward structures on faculty and in turn their research behavior (Tierney and Rhoads, 1994). Given the results of this study, it appears that research that is highly conceptual, methodologically sound, and descriptive; that raises questions; and that (to some degree) is creative is rewarded. Researchers seem not to be socialized to or rewarded for research that has relevance to practice, for good writing, for writing for an audience, for choosing an important topic, for being visionary, for being insightful, for providing perspective, for being solution oriented, for understanding the landscape of higher education, or for producing concise formats for practitioners. The field of higher education might be responding to a larger academic system that rewards an orientation to academic culture and a separation from practice.

After a review of these explanations and others (for example, research paradigm and disciplinary difference), a more systematic way to explain researchers' and practitioners' behavior emerged: the dichotomy between theory and practice is a social construction. This explanation suggests that the culture of the academy, the reward system of tenure, the socialization of faculty, the disciplinary orientations, and the unclear designation of higher education as a professional field or a discipline are all encompassed within a larger paradigm that discounts practice (or for practitioners, discounts research) and separates research from practice. Making this false dichotomy apparent would allow the field (both practitioners and researchers) to reconceptualize its value system and resolve the gap. The way to begin dissolving a false dichotomy is to create a new culture and socialize the field to a philosophy that emphasizes continuity and mutuality. This explanation implies that practitioners and researchers must work together and redefine the field of higher education. This strategy moves beyond the different culture or role explanations that continue to reinforce that these groups exist in different worlds.

This study advances a new direction for addressing this problem—*mutuality and continuity*. A new language and philosophy are necessary to reshape and reframe the work of higher education professionals. Rather than continuing to focus on the gap, this volume suggests ways to move beyond this false dichotomy. This *New Directions* volume provides detailed descriptions of strategies that can develop a collaborative research process and continuity between the work of practitioners and researchers.

All of the strategies that follow in the next chapters rely on reshaping the way the higher education community conceptualizes work—from its day-to-day practice to annual rituals such as conferences. Through dialogue, researchers certainly can develop more relevant and useful research, and practitioners certainly can become more familiar with the resources available to them and can contribute to knowledge generation. It is possible to reshape the way the profession of higher education is framed. I hope that you will use these strategies and develop new ones to move us beyond the gap.

References

Dressel, P., and Mayhew, L. *Higher Education as a Field of Study*. San Francisco: Jossey-Bass, 1974.

Keller, G. "Does Higher Education Research Need Revisions?" *Review of Higher Education*, 1998, *21*(3), 267–278.
Tierney, W., and Rhoads, R. "Enhancing Promotions, Tenure, and Beyond." Washington, D.C.: ASHE-ERIC Higher Education Report, 1994, Vols. 22–26.

ADRIANNA KEZAR is assistant professor and director of the ERIC Clearinghouse on Higher Education at the George Washington University.

2

Reviewing the history of higher education as both a professional field and a disciplinary field assists in understanding the current relationship between researchers and practitioners. It is becoming increasingly critical to balance the competing interests of those who believe we should be orienting our research to the theoretical needs of the disciplines, to the canons of research, or to the practical requirements of practice and policy.

The Tyranny of Success: The Research-Practice Tension

Marvin W. Peterson

Achieving the appropriate balance of scholarship in an emerging field of professional study is always a source of tension. To what degree should the field of study reflect sound conceptual and theoretical links to other disciplines, address the concerns of its practitioner community, or engage in theory development and research that is unique to our field? Conducting scholarly inquiry and research that is sophisticated and relevant to each of these goals yet reflects the uniqueness of our emerging field and the interests of its members is a sensitive and difficult balancing act. The distinctions, though often subtle, have not escaped the study of higher education, and the gaps between or the tensions among our contributions to theory development, to research, and to practice may be widening. Consider four scenarios that reflect these distinctions:

- The higher education faculty had selected three finalists for an assistant professor to cover the public policy area—a very capable young doctoral recipient in political science who had focused his dissertation on a theoretical model of federal-state relations in higher education policy; a doctoral graduate from a reputable higher education center with a strong research emphasis and a primary focus in public policy of postsecondary education; and a highly respected analyst from a sophisticated state agency staff with strong practitioner ties to state higher education executive officers' offices and knowledge of federal programs (also with a doctorate).
- A senior higher education faculty member was debating three funding options for his scholarly efforts for the next two years—doing a pragmatic comparative study evaluating the efficacy of a state-sponsored diversity effort

at six public universities on a contract with the state governing board, considering the dean's encouragement to do a cross-institutional study of factors explaining the success of diversity programs in schools or colleges of education, or responding to a promising foundation overture to do a theoretical interpretation of the varied approaches to diversity in extant higher education research.

• The academic vice president of a major university had received encouragement to start a higher education–policy research initiative and was considering whether to have its primary affiliation with the university's well-respected higher education program, its strong political science department, or its practical but highly effective public policy institute or whether it was possible to create a new center that would seek collaboration with each.

• The national conference program committee of the Association for the Study of Higher Education (ASHE) wanted a keynote speaker on "Directions for Higher Education Scholarship in the Twenty-First Century" and debated the merits of inviting a widely respected university president with provocative ideas about the future of higher education, a renowned sociologist on the theory of knowledge development and its contribution to society, or a well-known educational researcher and past president of the American Educational Research Association (AERA) who is interested in emerging educational research methods.

These four vignettes reflect at the individual, departmental, university, and professional-association level the pressures within the field of higher education to orient our research to the theoretically inclined academic disciplines, to the canons of research methods in the emerging profession of higher education, or to the needs of practice and policy.

Purpose and Perspectives

The intent of this chapter is not to resolve the tensions among theory, research, and practice. It will not carefully classify, analyze, and synthesize our higher education research and its contributions. Rather it is an opportunity to reflect on our field's development and the emergence of the tensions around our research and its relations to theory, to methodology, and to practice. The chapter reflects my own experiences. I first became enmeshed in the debates about the nature of higher education as a field of study when, as a graduate student, I began attending meetings of professors of higher education in 1967.

My first perspective begins unabashedly with an assertion that higher education is now a recognized professional field of study—one that incorporates concepts and theories from many disciplinary and professional fields, has a sound record of research that uses varied methods and addresses diverse topics and issues, and has many potential practitioner and policy constituents—that on occasion even develops its own unique theories, research methods, and contributions to practice.

My second perspective is to look at our field from a systemic vantage point—to focus on the interaction between the field of higher education and four major constituent groups that have influenced or shaped the theory-research-practice balance in our scholarly efforts. The field of higher or postsecondary education consists of our professional associations and publications, our predominantly university-based programs and centers, our research priorities as reflected by our educational and scholarly work, and our primary participants—faculty and students in our higher education programs and centers. Three major external constituent groups that shape or influence our scholarly efforts are the academic disciplines and related professions, the larger profession of education, and the professional arena of postsecondary practice and policymaking. A fourth external group, funding sources, has a different relationship but is important to note.

My final perspective is to suggest that we are not really dealing with a research-to-practice dichotomy or gap, as other authors characterize it, but rather with a trichotomy—the relationship among our theory-research-practice orientation. Our scholarship or research can be driven by conceptual and theoretical models derived largely from other disciplines. We view this as being academically more legitimate, yet it makes our research sometimes less practical. Our scholarship or research can be driven by our own methodological and content interests (and I will argue that to some extent it has been), which may have limited conceptual generalizability or practical utility. Or our scholarship and research can be driven by the constantly changing needs or demands of practitioners—always too little, too late and often adding little to our conceptual understanding of higher education as a field. As members of a professional field with our own specific setting, we always struggle with the right balance. We can develop our own unique theories and methods for the problems of higher education, or we can be guided by the theories and concepts of the disciplines. We can be driven by our own internal methodological and topical interests, or we can be dominated by the needs of practice and policymaking.

Viewing higher education as an emerging professional field subjected to the four external forces discussed previously, it is useful for us to ponder a question that draws from institutional and resource dependence theory: Is the field of higher education, in seeking legitimacy, subject to the same pattern of isomorphism that affects the disciplines and autonomous professions and that leads to isolation from practice, or is higher education so resource and politically dependent on the research pressures of the field, the priorities of its funding sources, and the interests of policymakers and practitioners that it is dominated by or subsumed by them?

The purpose of the remainder of this chapter is threefold—to reflect on our development as a professional field, to speculate on some key pressures from the four sources that are shaping the scholarship of our field, and to identify some focused research questions that may guide us in understanding this trichotomous tension of theory-research-practice. Before examining the interface between the field of higher education and its external environment, it is useful to reflect on our development to date.

Development as a Profession: Success and Isolation

By any standard, higher education has emerged as a successful professional field over the past four decades. But has that success also bred isolation from our disciplinary and practitioner worlds? There is ample evidence of roots for the study of higher education prior to World War II, but its development as a professional field is largely a postwar phenomenon. Beginning in the late 1950s and throughout the 1960s, a small group of faculty met regularly on Sunday afternoons preceding the annual American Association for Higher Education (AAHE) Conference. In the late 1950s, with higher education expanding rapidly in enrollment and numbers of institutions, The Carnegie Foundation funded centers for the study of higher education at Berkeley, Michigan, and Columbia to foster research, professional development for administrators, and graduate training in higher education. The W. K. Kellogg Foundation joined in shortly thereafter to support efforts to assist the exploding community college arena. These would serve as models, stimulating the development of programs and centers elsewhere to offer graduate teaching, research, and service in higher education. In the early 1970s when AAHE was no longer willing to assist the higher education faculty with their special meeting, the Association of Professions of Higher Education—the precursor to ASHE—was formed. Debates about the nature of higher education as a field, the need for and the role of research, and the design of graduate programs dominated the agenda.

Throughout this early period and extending well into the 1970s, there were strong ties between the new scholars and faculty in higher education and both the disciplines and the administrative and policy leaders. The reasons were obvious. Most new higher education faculty came from disciplines where they were respected and active or from prior administrative leadership roles (for example, from Stanford, Hal Cowley and Nevitt Sanford, both in psychology; from Berkeley, T. R. McConnell in psychology, Harold Hodgkinson and Burton Clark in sociology, Lyman Glenny in political science; from Columbia, Earl McGrath in humanities; from Michigan, Algo Henderson, former president of Antioch, in law and business administration, John Brubacher in law and philosophy; from Pennsylvania State, G. Lester Anderson, former president of the University of Buffalo; and the list goes on). Higher education faculty were regularly featured speakers at their disciplinary associations and at administrative association meetings such as AAHE and the American Council on Education (ACE). Several scholarly oriented administrators, such as Chancellor Clark Kerr at University of California-Berkeley; President James Perkins at Cornell University; John Millett, head of the Ohio Board of Regents; and Howard Bowen, president at Grinnell and Iowa, among others, contributed key books to the higher education literature. This was clearly an era in which higher education faculty were well known to the presidents on their own campuses and were active in their disciplinary fields, and higher education executive officers were interested in the emerging scholarship that helped them understand their students and manage or govern their growing institutions. New higher education faculty, faculty from the disciplines, and administrators were all contributing to an emerging literature on higher education. The theory-research-practice gaps may have existed, but disciplines, higher education faculty, and administrators were all contributing to the emergence of the field of higher education and for the most part were communicating. Indeed an informal, self-perpetuating higher education colloquium, which consisted equally of faculty and researchers in higher education and administrators and policymakers with a scholarly interest in higher education issues, was formed and met regularly at AAHE and ACE to discuss emergent research and critical issues. By the 1990s, this group found it impossible to find a professional meeting where both higher education faculty and administrators attend in significant numbers. It now meets only at ASHE— a conference attended mostly by higher education scholars. Few, if any, administrators or policymakers attend.

From the mid-1970s and extending through the 1980s, the field of higher education developed rapidly. New programs in higher education emerged in many universities. New faculty were increasingly being hired from among the graduates of the more established doctoral programs in higher education. The "cloning" process had begun. ASHE became a stable organization with its own national office and successful annual conference. AERA formed Division J on postsecondary education. ASHE sponsored a new journal, the *Review of Higher Education,* which joined the previously established AAHE-affiliated *Journal of Higher Education* and the Association for Institutional Research–sponsored *Research in Higher Education* to provide three scholarly and research-oriented publications to serve the field. The AAHE-ERIC *Research Report Series,* which focused primarily on disseminating higher education research to practitioners, became an ASHE-ERIC–sponsored series.

Primary issues, within ASHE and at our national conference, shifted from the nature of the field to more internal issues during the 1980s. The 1983 ASHE conference, where I served as president and program chair, featured three speakers who were funded by a Ford Foundation grant and who addressed the links of higher education to the social sciences (Professor James March of Stanford University), the humanities (Professor Walter Metzger at Columbia University), and the futurists (Michael Marien of the World Futures Society). After that, debates on the nature of the field diminished. They then shifted to issues of inclusiveness of graduate students and minority members and on new research methods and paradigms.

By the 1990s, the field of higher education could be considered well established. The two primary associations, ASHE and AERA-Division J, are stable and growing. ASHE, with around twelve hundred members, focuses on the broad range of educational and scholarly issues faced by higher education programs and centers, sponsors both the scholarly *Review of Higher Education* and the more practice-oriented ASHE-ERIC *Research Report Series,* and publishes the ASHE Reader series. AERA-Division J, with about eight hundred members, focuses more narrowly on research and the relationship of higher and postsecondary education to the larger education community. There are now over a hundred higher education graduate programs or research centers listed in the most recent ASHE directory. They are varied in size, focus, and research-practice orientation but cover all areas of the study of higher education, and some have affiliated research units. Most of these are now directed by individuals with doctoral degrees in higher education, and new hires are almost always graduates of higher education programs.

The professionalization process of the field has progressed substantially—but so has the process of isolation. Higher education faculty are far less visible in other disciplines and professions and are largely absent from professional administrative associations, where they were formerly active. (Exceptions are AIR, which has an active special-interest group for faculty, and AAHE and the National Association of Student Personnel Administrators, which still attract some higher education faculty. All, however, are small and have specialized interests reflecting the association.) Debates in ASHE about relationships with the disciplines and other professional fields are largely dormant, and our earlier arguments about research methods have subsided. Only the concern about the relationship of our scholarship to practice and policymaking, raised in Patrick Terenzini's 1995 ASHE presidential address (1996) and discussed by Adrianna Kezar in the opening chapter of this volume, dominates our debates about the nature of the field now, as we enter the 2000s. Has our own drive for professional success as an emerging field isolated us from our multidisciplinary past and our policy and practitioner colleagues, or is our isolation the result of other forces? A brief look at some of these forces may provide insight.

Contextual Forces

It is useful to reflect on the contextual changes in our primary constituent groups that have shaped our research and our relationship to them during the four decades of higher education's maturation as a professional field. Many come to mind, but four that I consider critical are discussed here.

Growth of Administrative Complexity. The close relationship between early higher education faculty and key administrators and policymakers was a product both of who the early faculty were (respected senior faculty or former administrators) and of simpler times. Institutions in the 1950s and 1960s were smaller, and so were the administrative staffs who supported senior officers. During the struggle to deal with these institutions as they were growing, it was only natural to turn to senior faculty who were interested in similar issues. However, the need for better managerial information and research on institutional problems, processes, and issues led to a rapid expansion in the field of institutional research in the 1960s. In a national study, Rourke and Brooks (1966) called it *The Managerial Revolution*. This new function would add a cadre of applied researchers to most institutional administrations by 1980. The challenge of managing larger institutions and the increasingly demanding competitive and political pressures would lead to the proliferation of assistant, associate, and assistant-to positions for the president and other senior executive officers, which provided them with a staff resource to summarize higher education research and to serve as a buffer between the executive officers and the faculty. This growth of middle-level administrators, which exceeded that of faculty and students, is well documented (Anderson and others, 1989). By 1980, the period of growth and expansion of higher education that fueled the managerial revolution had subsided. As institutions began to focus on living with constrained enrollments and finances, they began to look for ways to respond to calls for academic accountability. In the late 1980s, the emphasis shifted from institutional management to academic management. This expansion of academic support services, program and faculty evaluation efforts, and faculty and instructional support offices was called the "Academic Management Revolution" (Peterson, 1990). The trend continues in the 1990s with the growth of the "Assessment Revolution" (Peterson, 1999) and the expansion of offices to assist with all forms of student, faculty, and academic assessment and studies of factors influencing student and academic performance.

This expansion was not limited to the campus. The 1960s and 1970s witnessed the formation and expansion of multicampus system offices and state coordinating and governing boards with sizable staff—many dedicated to analytical or applied research functions and trained in higher education programs (Berdahl, 1971; Glenny, 1959). Simultaneously, professional administrative associations of all types were becoming more formalized and sophisticated. In order to provide services to their own individual or institutional members, these administrative associations added programs, services, and staff. By the 1980s, many were actively courting foundations for funding—often to support applied research as well as to provide training and developmental services to members.

This growth of administrative complexity was a two-edged sword in the field of higher education's expansion. It created an ever expanding market for graduates of higher education programs while also creating a large institutional administrative group of applied researchers or research synthesizers, who could more directly serve the needs of decision makers and policymakers. Administrative associations, often staffed by graduates of higher education programs, were often producing their own applied research and competing with higher education scholars for funds. Higher education's success was also contributing in part to constituents' analytical capacity and to the field's increasing isolation from key leaders' constituents.

Unwilling Captives. It can be argued that a second major factor that contributed to higher education's isolation both from the disciplines and from practice was that higher education programs became increasingly housed in colleges and schools of education. Because early founders of higher education programs and centers were from the disciplines, their units often had a good deal of autonomy. But by the mid-1970s, most programs were being subsumed into schools of education—sometimes as a separate department or unit but more often as a small program within a larger department. Although this development strengthened the relationship with the broader field of education, it also probably served to widen the gap between higher education and both the disciplines and the world of practice and policy. The lower academic status and salary levels of individuals in education departments compared with individuals in other departments in many research and doctoral universities have made it more difficult to hire faculty with disciplinary-based degrees, to gain access to senior administrators, or to mount joint efforts with other units. The mere size of most higher education faculty groups also put them at a political disadvantage in the larger K–12-oriented departments and schools.

A less visible but significant consequence of the shifting of the locus of higher education programs may be its impact on the nature of their scholarship. Students were less likely to obtain more theoretically oriented, discipline-based course work and rigorous research training. Younger faculty, driven by lesser research standards and relying on publishing articles in education-related journals, have focused on narrow, specific research projects rather than on research of broad issues (appropriate to publication in books). This was reflected in the criticism raised by Cameron (1985), who contended that articles published in higher education journals were on narrowly focused research topics and did not address major issues of concern to top administrators. Keller's (1985) article, "Trees Without Fruit," argued that higher education research did not make significant contributions in the aggregate to either theory or practice. This was the basis for a lively panel at the ASHE National Conference in San Antonio in 1983.

The dilemma, of course, is that a program's locus strengthens its potential linkage to one important external constituent—the field of education—but makes its scholarly contribution to practice and its theoretical or conceptual link to disciplines more difficult. These concerns notwithstanding, it is clear that some higher education units have managed to do one or both (link their research to practice or research to theory) by building a strong core faculty, organizing as a separate academic unit, establishing an affiliated research center, or emphasizing research training and cognate work for their students.

Academic Insularity and the Paradigm Wars. Higher education's relationship to the disciplines and to related professional fields also has been a two-edged sword. As the early wave of discipline-trained faculty retired and were increasingly replaced by higher education faculty, the difficulty in maintaining strong relationships with theoretical developments and research efforts in the disciplines became more complicated.

At the same time, many disciplines and professional groups have themselves become more insular. In addition, their interest in higher education as an arena for study or as a group with whom to collaborate has been episodic, depending on what is happening in higher education at a given time. For example, in the 1960s and 1970s, political scientists were quite interested in higher education when state coordination and governance were in a state of flux, but interests lagged when those conditions stabilized. Economists were more interested in the early 1970s when federal financial aid changed drastically and the economic recession was affecting higher education institutions. Sociologists and psychologists rekindled some of their interests during the period of student dissidence in the late 1960s and early 1970s and again in the 1990s and now the 2000s, as diversity issues have become prominent.

In addition, ASHE, AERA-Division J, and the field of higher education were not immune from the conflicts over research approaches. The conflicts over research paradigms that were waged as ideological holy wars in the disciplines in the 1970s and early 1980s eventually reached higher education in the late 1980s and early 1990s, as qualitative and quantitative methods were debated. These debates tended to be divisive within the field of higher education and may have complicated our attempts to relate to practitioners. The level of the debate prompted Pascarella to focus his ASHE presidential address in 1990 on the paradigm wars in ASHE and to attempt to bridge the gap between the quantitative, qualitative, and postmodern camps. We often forget that thanks to our early discipline-based faculty, many conceptual perspectives and many methods have always been part of our higher education heritage. Historical, ethnographic, case study, comparative, and survey methods using quantitative and qualitative approaches all have examples in higher education studies dating from the 1960s. And some of the most influential studies and scholarly syntheses have used multiple methods or have examined studies using many different methods.

The challenges for higher education research are to recognize the various disciplinary contributions to our field, to avoid overly narrow topics and insignificant or transient practical issues, and to avoid becoming captives of our methods rather than valuing alternative methods for what each of them tells us. If we address significant, practical, or conceptual issues with appropriate or multiple methods and do them well, the primary issue is how to communicate to disciplinary scholars, to higher education colleagues, and to practitioners.

Funding Sources. Perhaps as much as any other constituent group, funding sources influence the link of our scholarship to theory and to practice. Like education in general, higher education has had little sustained or large-scale research funding. Foundations and the federal government are the two primary resources external to our universities that have supported higher education research and each deserve brief comment.

The Carnegie Foundation's grants in the 1950s, which established the centers for the study of higher education at Berkeley, Michigan, and Columbia, were a major infusion and laid the groundwork for later research funding. However, those funds went primarily toward the establishment of the centers—not to the direct support of research. Although The Carnegie Foundation funded some research projects in the early years, its best known effort was funding the work of The Carnegie Commission on Higher Education from 1967–1972 under the direction of Clark Kerr. The massive effort of The Carnegie Commission provided perhaps the best example of a research effort that enhanced our knowledge of higher education at one point in time, involved disciplinary as well as higher education researchers, and influenced or shaped the views of institutional leaders and policymakers. The foundation ultimately provided The Carnegie Foundation for the Advancement of Teaching with an endowment to carry on research in that area. The Carnegie Foundation for the Advancement of Teaching, first under the direction of Ernest Boyer and now Lee Shulman, has produced several works that have shaped the broader field of higher education's work on teaching and the nature of scholarship and that have been well received by institutional leaders. However, both The Carnegie Foundation for the Advancement of Teaching and The Carnegie Commission were efforts of groups that were outside the university-based programs and centers. The Carnegie Foundation itself has now withdrawn from funding higher education research except that carried out by The Carnegie Foundation for the Advancement of Teaching.

Other notable foundations have provided some support for higher education research over the years. The Exxon Foundation, at an early period, supported research that addressed institutional problems. The Ford Foundation, periodically, has provided research support that addressed broader social issues in higher education. The Lilly Foundation provided research on liberal education and minority education issues until retreating to focus primarily on the state of Indiana. All of these addressed practical problems with little concern for theory. Only the Spencer Foundation has focused its support on theoretically based research or theory development. However, most of their support is for K–12-oriented work. The Pew Foundation, most recently, has begun focusing on issues related to improving student performance. Most other major foundations supporting higher education have focused on development and improvement efforts or on facilities rather than on research-based efforts. But overall the foundations have not provided continuing support over a long period, have often funded small-to-moderate projects, and usually have been focused on current problems or issues.

The federal government has had a more sustained but controversial record in supporting higher education research. Periodically, the National Institutes of Health, the National Institute of Mental Health, and the National Science Foundation (NSF) have sponsored research that focused on understanding some aspect of higher education, but they have been inconsistent. The Department of Education (DOE) (formerly the Office of Education) has been a major supporter of data collection on higher education through the National Center for Education Statistics (NCES). DOE's Office of Educational Research and Improvement, along with its precursor, the National Institute of Education, has been a primary sponsor of research on education, with only a small fraction focused on higher education. Although a small part of their higher education research has been through an open grants competition, most has been channeled through its sponsorship of national research-and-development centers with longer-term funding. Recently, NCES has taken significant steps to provide higher education researchers and graduate students access to extensive national data sets on students, faculty, and institutions. NSF has made similar efforts for their national data sets, which are related to postsecondary education in the areas of science and technology. Both provide training on quantitative research on national issues using these databases. The impact of this on theory development and on practice-oriented research remains to be seen.

The support of R&D centers over the past thirty years has been the most consistent form of federal support for research in the field of higher education. It has supported large-scale efforts that have encouraged both theory development and practical useful research within a context of current national problems and priorities. From 1965 to 1971, the Center for Higher Education Research and Development at Berkeley focused on studies of student development, innovation and institutional governance, and state coordination and policy. From 1971 to 1985, the National Center for Higher Education Management Systems, which was not university-based, designed and developed management information and analysis systems and conducted research on organizational effectiveness and strategy. From 1986–1991, the National Center for Research to Improve Postsecondary Teaching and Learning at the University of Michigan addressed issues of curriculum, instruction, technology, faculty behavior, and organizational support for teaching and learning. During the same period, the National Center for Governance and Finance at the University of Maryland examined a variety of organizational, governance, finance, and productivity issues. Between 1991 and 1996, the National Center for Teaching, Learning, and Assessment was based at the Pennsylvania State University, adding the focus on assessment. Most recently, the National Center for Postsecondary Improvement headquartered at Stanford University is examining changing patterns of institutional markets, college-to-work experiences, support for and uses of assessment, and organization-environment relations. The focus of these center efforts reflect differing higher education priorities over three decades, have to varying degrees involved some disciplinary as well as higher education scholars, have been theoretically based, and have had broad practice and policy implications. Their actual impact on scholarly development and on practice or policymaking, however, is often debated and has not been systematically evaluated.

The contributions of these funding sources and patterns are difficult to assess. Clearly, the federal efforts have provided some large-scale, longer-term funding on significant issues. But this was usually limited to a small group of scholars at any point in time. Most of the other efforts have been focused on specific issues that have policy and practice implications. With the exception of the R&D centers, there is little overt emphasis on theory development or on strengthening higher education's link to the disciplines and related professions.

Isolation or Integration: A Research Agenda

From this brief overview, it is clear that the field of higher education has emerged as a strong professional area of study. It has grown rapidly in numbers of programs, faculty, and students; has developed two successful and somewhat different professional associations; and has sponsored a set of strong professional journals dedicated to the field. But the field may be becoming isolated. We are mostly located in subunits of schools of education, primarily hire our own graduates, attend the same higher education association meetings, have fewer direct ties to faculty from other disciplines, are buffered from our institutional and policy leaders, are less active in other disciplinary and practitioner associations, and belong to associations that do not collaborate with other associations, with the exception of AERA. Many of these conditions are the result of the changes in or the influences of the major external constituents to the field of higher education, as well as of our own attempts to legitimize our field as a profession.

The temptation is to make a series of recommendations at the association, institution, program, and individual levels for bridging or maintaining our scholarly and research links to the conceptual world of our related disciplines and the primary practitioner and policymaking groups that we seek to understand and influence. But I would suggest that we need to seek a balance between the autonomy for the research and scholarship on higher education and the appropriate relationships with the discipline and with practice. To do so, we might more carefully examine or research the developments that are suggested in my perspective and reflections. We could use a careful examination of the following issues:

The scholarly and theoretical developments that have shaped the field of higher education—both those borrowed from the disciplines and those original or unique to our field

The influence of our higher education research and scholarship on policy

and practice in specific areas, such as state and federal policy, institutional governance, curriculum and instruction, student development and performance, faculty behavior, and economic benefits
The extent and nature of our field's professional involvement with relevant academic disciplines and related professional fields of study and with the professional practice and policymaking associations

At the higher education program-center-department level, we might ask a series of similar questions.

What is our theory-versus-practice emphasis, and what is the specific orientation of our program, our faculty expertise, and our research?
What are our links to the disciplines or other professional academic units on our campuses and to their national associations?
What are our links to administrative leadership and policymaking groups on our campuses and to their professional associations?

Each faculty member might ask the same questions of himself or herself. Only then can we begin to assess whether we are captives of our own success. Are we isomorphic slaves to legitimizing our own professional field and existence—isolated from related disciplines and from practitioners and policymakers? Or are we capable of achieving a balance and a desirable level of collaboration with relevant related disciplines, making a contribution to the larger field of education, and providing a base for sound policy and practice? Understanding the emergence of our field of higher education, its ever changing context, and the choices we are making to balance our relationships will be key to whether we become further isolated, further subsumed, or instead achieve an appropriate level of autonomy and interaction with our educational, disciplinary, and practitioner colleagues.

But the assessment of our status as a profession, as graduate programs, and as scholars in the field is not sufficient. Clearly, there are many challenges facing higher education at the start of the twenty-first century—new information and communication technologies; continued concerns for diversity; the growth of technology-based knowledge-delivery systems; demands to contribute to economic development; new postsecondary relearning or lifelong learning markets; concerns about cost, quality, and access; and the impact of globalization. The list goes on. Higher education, as we know it, is subject to tremendous demands to respond and to change—even to transform—our institutions, our delivery patterns, and our models of teaching and learning. In such an environment, scholarship, which is isolated from these demands, will be limiting. Assessing our field and its programs is only a strategy for setting the agenda. Addressing the new challenges to higher education, I expect, will require new modes of interacting with the disciplines and the higher education professional community we serve and new modes of research that will benefit from better links to both the worlds of theory and practice. The need to balance the theory-research-practice tension needs to be addressed to ensure that the field of higher education continues to be a vital force.

References

Anderson, C. J., and others. *1989–90 Factbook on Higher Education*. Washington, D.C.: American Council on Education, 1989.

Berdahl, R. *Statewide Coordination of Higher Education*. Washington, D.C.: American Council on Higher Education, 1971.

Cameron, K. Boulder, Colo.: National Center for Higher Education Management Systems, 1985.

Glenny, L. *The Autonomy of Public Colleges*. New York: McGraw-Hill, 1959.

Keller, G. "Trees Without Fruit: The Problem with Research About Higher Education." *Change*, 1985, (1), 7–10.

Peterson, M. W. *Assessing the Organizational and Administrative Context for Teaching and Learning*. Ann Arbor: National Center for Research to Improve Teaching and Learning, University of Michigan, 1990.

Peterson, M. W. "Revolution or Evolution? Gauging the Impact of Institutional Student Assessment Strategies." Sept.–Oct. 1999, 53.

Rourke, F. E., and Brooks, G. E. *The Managerial Revolution in Higher Education*. Baltimore: Johns Hopkins University Press, 1966.

Terenzini, P. T. "Rediscovering Roots: Public Policy and Higher Education Research." *Review of Higher Education*, 1996, (1), 5–13.

MARVIN W. PETERSON *is professor of higher education at the Center for the Study of Higher and Postsecondary Education at the University of Michigan.*

3

A myriad of forces influence faculty and the production of research, including tenure and promotion policies and practices, institutional socialization, disciplinary culture, and journal editors and senior scholars. These powerful forces must be rethought and reshaped if we are to bridge the research-practice gap.

Reshaping the Forces That Perpetuate the Research-Practice Gap: Focus on New Faculty

Carol L. Colbeck

Rhetoric about higher education crises, agendas, solutions, and problems reverberates in state legislatures, faculty senate meetings, and administrative edicts. Debate about higher education issues also consumes ink in the popular press, policy reports, scholarly journals, and managerial magazines, and now it also occupies cyberspace on the Internet. Despite all the verbiage, higher education administrators, policymakers, students, their parents, faculty, and the public apparently do not listen much to higher education scholars, and higher education scholars do not listen much to their stakeholders (Conrad, 1989; Keller, 1985; Terenzini, 1996). Kezar's research (see Chapter One) indicates that higher education scholars do not even listen much to one another. The communication gap between higher education scholars and stakeholders is particularly frustrating for new faculty who entered an applied field with hopes higher than attaining tenure—hopes that their scholarly efforts might somehow make a positive impact on the people, policies, and practice of higher education.

As a graduate student and assistant professor of higher education at two research universities, I have seen university administrators implement major teaching and curriculum reform initiatives without so much as brief phone consultations with experts on their own campuses who are renowned for their research in those areas. I have also heard education professors hesitate to offer their expertise to administrators, either doubting that their counsel would be heeded or fearful that administrative requests for institutional research would become yet another unrecognized requirement of higher education faculty members' demanding jobs. But I have also learned much from opportunities to work closely with senior scholars who consistently and creatively integrate educational research and practice.

With those lessons in mind, I argue in this chapter that there are ways that tenure-seeking faculty in higher education can bridge the research-practice gap. Well-directed efforts to improve communication among higher education scholars, practitioners, and policymakers might improve junior faculty chances for attaining tenure. Such efforts, which include active listening and reciprocal relationship, may also be the catalysts required to revitalize a relatively young field of study that has already been labeled lifeless and pedestrian (Conrad, 1989), picayune (Keller, 1985), and narrow (Terenzini, 1996) by some of its leading scholars.

First, I explore the professionalization and socialization forces that encourage new faculty to perpetuate the research-practice gap in higher education. Next, I suggest alternative ways to view the relationship among higher education scholars, practitioners, and policymakers, drawing on communication theory, feminist philosophy, and organizational theory. Finally, I offer recommendations for ways that junior faculty can bridge the gap and ways that senior faculty and administrators can support their efforts, to the collective benefit of all.

Forces That Encourage New Faculty to Perpetuate the Gap

New higher education faculty are caught between experiences that are likely to help them bridge the research-practice gap and socializing forces that encourage them to reinforce the gap. It is likely that a majority of higher education faculty were practitioners before they were scholars, as more than three-fourths of the graduates of higher education doctoral programs worked at colleges, universities, or related agencies before starting doctoral study (Townsend and Weise, 1991). It is also likely that many assistant professors have graduate school colleagues who have become practitioners, as a majority of those who hold doctorates in higher education work as middle-level or senior-level college or university administrators in agencies focusing on higher education (Townsend and Weise, 1991). Furthermore, as the number of faculty who staff a higher education program on any campus is comparatively few, most of any new faculty member's campus colleagues are administrators and faculty in other fields or disciplines—in other words, practitioners.

Although assistant professors of higher education may have had practical experience and do have friends and colleagues who are higher education practitioners, new faculty quickly learn that their new profession requires that they establish separate identities as scholars. When they were still graduate students, they began learning the values of the education professoriate from their teachers and mentors. Little of that learning was likely to have involved lessons in the worth of reciprocal communication with practitioners and policymakers (Peterson, 1998; Miller, 1999; Terenzini, 1996) or acknowledgement that by nature of their positions as faculty members, higher education scholars are also practitioners. Although some senior scholars assert that the research-practice gap should be bridged (Conrad, 1989; Keller, 1985; Terenzini, 1996; Hearn, 1998), others emphasize the differences rather than the similarities between scholars and practitioners or policymakers (Birnbaum, 2000).

Research on the process of professionalization in other fields helps explain why some higher education scholars distance themselves from practitioners. One of the hallmarks of achieving professional status is the general perception that certified members of the profession have developed expertise in a body of knowledge and a set of skills obtained only through long and intensive education (Friedson, 1986). The perception of having expertise is facilitated by the development of professional jargon. There is "a social pressure on would-be professionals to create a closed and esoteric vocabulary" so they may claim a monopoly on their particular skills (Brown, 1992, p. 21). Higher education is certainly not the first young social science field to adopt scientific formats and "obfuscatory verbiage" (Conrad, 1989) to gain legitimacy among the community of scholars. In 1959, C. Wright Mills asserted that the unintelligibility of sociological writing "has little or nothing to do with the profundity of the subject matter, and has nothing at all to do with profundity of thought" (p. 218). He further described the origins of sociological jargon, "In large part sociological habits of style stem from the time when sociologists had little status even with other academic men. Desire for status is one reason why academic men slip so easily into unintelligibility" (p. 218). Unintelligibility is perpetuated as succeeding generations of scholars emulate the obtuse style of articles written by renowned scholars. Editors publish jargon-filled articles by new authors because nothing better is available and because copyediting is expensive. Those articles provide the examples from which the next generation learns bad habits (Becker, 1986).

Journal reviewers and editors are among the senior colleagues who play a critical gatekeeping role in the socialization of new higher education faculty. New scholars learn "notions of correctness," including "values, norms, and postures" from the comments of reviewers and editors (Silverman, 1993, p. 506). Correctness in higher education literature, as in much other academic writing, is "less an agent of intellectual change than a vehicle for maintaining social stability in the face of change" (Kaufer and Geisler, 1989, p. 287). In his content analysis of all articles published in the top five higher education journals from 1986–1988, Milam (1991) found that all articles were concerned with the status quo, and none offered innovative or visionary ideas that practitioners say would help them improve practice (see Kezar, Chapter One).

To bridge the research-practice gap by communicating with administrators, faculty in other disciplines, and policy analysts, as well as with other higher education scholars, new higher education faculty should begin doing so early in their careers. Scholars establish patterns for publication during their tenure-seeking years—not during graduate school nor after receiving promotion (Boice, 1992). Publication patterns involve the rate at which new faculty submit manuscripts, the topics about which they write, and the audiences for whom they publish. The length of time required for attaining tenure virtually ensures that faculty members' early publishing habits will endure. The high stakes involved in up-or-out tenure decisions discourage new faculty from taking intellectual risks that might involve questioning the status quo, exploring innovative research topics or methodologies, or even communicating effectively with practitioners (Dunn, Rouse, and Seff, 1994; Tierney and Bensimon, 1996).

Experiences of assistant professors in other applied fields illustrate the risks involved. If assistant professors play it safe by waiting to communicate with practitioners until after tenure, they risk suppressing their creative energy and potential contributions to practice and scholarship. If they are too eager to communicate with practitioners, their community of scholars may soon silence them by denying tenure. For example, junior faculty who observed senior organizations scholars discussing the benefits of research that is relevant for both research and management practice realized that until tenured, they could not afford the luxury of such research. "One young faculty member expressed a certain sadness that his short-term career dilemmas had become quite clear: for the present he must orient himself to an institutional reward structure that precludes dealing with the pressing organizational concern that led him to the field in the first place" (Goodman, 1985, p. 350). No doubt he wanted to avoid a fate similar to that of a tenure-seeking faculty member described by Tierney and Bensimon in their study of new faculty socialization. The assistant professor was denied tenure because his seventeen publications were primarily in professional-level journals. As his department chair said, "Articles written for a lay audience do not meet with great acceptance" (1996, p. 66).

The costs of communicating with the "lay audience" of practitioners have been high for some assistant professors of higher education, who have been told that their articles in Change, Academe, or Phi Delta Kappan would not be included in the count of publications for tenure. The costs of not listening to, speaking with, or writing for higher education stakeholders, however, may be far higher for all higher education scholars. As Patrick Terenzini said in his 1995 presidential address to the Association for the Study of Higher Education, "Engaging in more practice- and policy-oriented research is, I believe, both a professional responsibility and a self-interested necessity. In the current financial climate, accountability driven as it is, we cannot expect continued public support for research that does not serve public needs" (1996, p. 8).

Communication to Bridge the Research-Practice Gap

According to Kezar's research (see Chapter One), one reason why practitioners seldom consult higher education literature is because publications typically report the current state of the academy but do not offer visions for the future. Visionary perspectives are needed if we are to bridge the research-practice gap. Socialization and professionalization theories help explain why current efforts to bridge the gap may fall short. With help from colleagues who are both scholars *and* practitioners, I found visionary perspectives about how to bridge the gap in applied communication theories (Gudykunst, 1998; Bolton, 1990), in a feminist philosophy of listening (Fiumara, 1990), and in the experiences of organizations scholars who had dealt with their own research-practice gap in the 1980s (Lawler and Associates, 1985).

Communication involves the creation of meaning as people exchange messages. There is no guarantee, however, that the people involved interpret the exchange in the same way. Therefore, "Communication is effective to the extent that the person interpreting the message attaches a meaning to the message similar to what was intended by the person transmitting it" (Gudykunst, 1998, p. 27). To increase the chances for effective communication requires listening, being open to new information, and being aware of more than one perspective when speaking (Bolton, 1990). Much scholarship, however, involves one-way communication, lecturing, rather than two-way communication, speaking *and* listening (Fiumara, 1990). In addition to content delivery and attention paid to how that content is interpreted, effective communication involves a relationship dimension that is inferred from how the messages are transmitted (Gudykunst, 1998). In the following sections, I explore how the concepts of listening and relationship may help new higher education faculty engage in research that informs both higher education theory and practice.

Listening. Despite the importance of listening and of being heard, "Whole disciplines are dedicated to the development and analysis of writing and of speaking and only marginal attention is paid to the reader and almost none to the listener," according to a recently retired academic administrator (Melander, 1999, p. 7). Listening involves trying to understand a speaker's perspectives and checking to see if one's perceptions of what the speaker said are accurate (Gudykunst, 1998). According to Italian feminist philosopher G. C. Fiumara (1990), "There could be no saying without hearing, no speaking which is not also an integral part of listening, no speech which is not somehow received" (p. 1). Failure to listen to one another throughout the academy may foster unnecessary and perhaps dysfunctional differences. Failure to listen also leads to stagnation of creative thought, which leads to research that must inevitably focus on the status quo. When we scholars do not listen, Fiumara says, "We can no longer share in 'creative thinking,' and we must confine ourselves more and more to circulating within a given repertory, or arsenal, of terms and standard articulations, which can be summoned up each time in mnemonic fashion; almost a pledge to comply with standard ways of mirroring and with reproductive thinking" (pp. 166–167).

If failing to listen leads to division and stagnation, then engaging in *active listening* may promote understanding and innovation. Actively listening to practitioners is likely to help new higher education scholars develop or expand their research agendas. When Kezar (Chapter One) recently asked focus groups of higher education scholars to discuss what were current important issues that should be investigated, few offered concrete ideas. When asked the same question, practitioners in the focus groups suggested many specific topics. The focus of practitioners' work is dealing successfully—or at least adequately—with current issues. When a fraternity pledge dies of alcohol poisoning, the dean of student affairs not only must cope with the current crises but also must consider how similar tragedies can be prevented. When a private liberal arts college president learns that enrollments have declined for the third year in a row, she not only must figure how to balance this year's budget but also must figure how to improve yields in subsequent years and how to generate alternative sources of revenue. When an assistant professor in mechanical engineering is assigned to teach a new freshman design course that includes group projects, she not only must design a syllabus but also must determine how she will assess students' design and team competencies at the end of the course to meet new engineering accreditation requirements. Listening to these practitioners, new higher education scholars can hear many important problems that would benefit from theory-driven investigation or evaluation (Chen and Rossi, 1983). Some organizational theorists have already realized that innovative scholarship results from listening to and learning from the expertise of managers and other organizational participants. For example, Lawler said, "In traditional scientific research the assumption is that expertise about the phenomenon being studied rests with the research scientist, not with the subject of the research. In most cases this is a safe assumption. But is it a safe assumption with respect to organizations and individual behavior in organizations? . . . Often managers and organization members are astute observers of the situation they are in, and their innovations in practice often precede theory" (1985, p. 6). Higher education practitioners and policymakers *are* astute observers, and new scholars can learn about fruitful areas for research from listening to their concerns and challenges.

Listening to practitioners' and policymakers' plans and hopes may also help assistant professors of higher education envision research ideas and conduct studies with a visionary rather than a retrospective focus. Organizations scholar Richard Hackman asserted that advancements in organizational theorizing are more likely to occur when scholars listen to managers and other organizational participants and then engage in application-focused research. Reflecting on the development of other social science disciplines, such as experimental psychology, Hackman said, "It may be that the best way to generate advances in basic theory is to do research that seeks solutions to real problems and to keep one's eyes open for fundamental conceptual issues as one proceeds" (1985, pp. 146–147).

Building Reciprocal Relationships. The process of active listening promotes understanding and reciprocal relationship, even if it does not always—and should not always—promote agreement. The relationship between educational research and practice involves negotiation and dialogue (Peterson, 1998). According to Fiumara, "In recognizing the deeply interactive nature of every dialogue we discover that we share in both the problem and the solution without being able to escape into neutral and unrelated spaces" (1990, p. 190). Although there may be some utility in enumerating the differences between higher education scholars and practitioners (Birnbaum, 2000), innovative and rewarding partnerships between scholars and practitioners are more likely to result from focusing on the similarities between them. Organizational theorist Andrew Pettigrew (1985) observed that many good research skills are similar to good management practices. Scholars and practitioners both attack major problems, engage in constant intervention, have developed depth and breadth of knowledge, sometimes act with incomplete data using their experience and intuition, and ask for help when confused.

Similarity extends to identity when considering higher education scholars and practitioners. As instructors, higher education professors deal with issues of teaching and learning in their own classrooms. As members of department and university committees and senates, they deal with issues of organization and leadership. As employees, they are dependent on the financial health of their colleges, universities, and state systems. As members of the larger higher education community, scholars must personally confront issues of equity, access, quality, and accountability. Higher education policy scholar James Hearn acknowledged that "higher education is not only our area of expertise, but also our area of livelihood" (1998, p. 2). The research-practice gap is more likely to narrow when more higher education scholars recognize that they are also higher education practitioners.

Just as the concept of active listening reveals that practitioners can be a valuable source of research ideas, the concept of building relationship reveals the importance of speaking and writing in ways that are clear to practitioner colleagues as well as to scholars. Mutual respect on the part of scholars, practitioners, policymakers, and stakeholders is necessary if they are to work together to develop and conduct research that advances theory and improves practice (Hackman, 1985). Both critics and proponents of efforts to write for practitioners have characterized the process as "simplifying" technical analysis and specialized language for lay audiences who lack scholars' expertise (Birnbaum, 2000; McColl and White, 1998). Hearn points out, however, that underestimating colleagues' ability to understand complex issues can work both ways, "Just as policy makers may tend to oversimplify policy *issues,* those from higher education may tend to oversimplify policy *making* itself" (emphasis added; 1998, p. 4).

When serving as members of faculty senates and university committees, higher education scholars often manage to communicate effectively with chemists, historians, engineers, linguists, deans of student affairs, and finance officers about college and university issues. Using similar clear communication techniques to explain their theories and research results is more likely to enhance rather than reduce higher education researchers' credibility with many of their scholarly and practitioner colleagues (Becker, 1986; Conrad, 1989; McColl and White, 1998).

Recommendations

Several leading higher education scholars have eloquently encouraged colleagues to bridge the research-practice gap (Conrad, 1989; Keller, 1985; Terenzini, 1996; Hearn, 1998). In this chapter, I have argued that although bridging the gap can be very risky for tenure-seeking faculty, the process can also provide them with meaningful topics to investigate, access to data, and better understanding of the utility of their research. New faculty can take some steps to bridge the gap even with minimal support from senior colleagues. Assistant professors willing to take the career risks, however, should have moral and practical support from the journal editors, senior higher education scholars, and practitioners who are likely to benefit from junior scholars' efforts. These recommendations are based on the literatures, my own experiences as an assistant professor of higher education, and on countless conversations on this subject with junior and senior colleagues, both faculty and administrators.

New Faculty. Developing professional friendships and working relationships with colleagues beyond the higher education scholarly community is the first step tenure-seeking faculty can take toward bridging the research-practice gap. Faculty who spend as much time networking with colleagues as they do on writing are among the most productive scholars (Boice, 1992; Creswell, 1985). If they do so nowhere else, new higher education faculty meet professors and administrators outside their departments when serving on university task forces or dissertation committees. By asking such colleagues to share conversation over lunch or a cup of coffee, new faculty can create opportunities to listen and learn about current important issues from practitioners. Such relationships can lead to opportunities to conduct theory-based evaluations of teaching, curricular, or administrative innovations on campus (Chen and Rossi, 1983). The next step involves integrating research with one's teaching or university service (Colbeck, 1998). Maintaining a participant-observer's perspective when serving on college and university committees enables a new faculty member to consider and develop researchable questions even while engaging in required service to the institution. Depending on the political climate at one's own institution, it may be possible to conduct such research on site, or it may be advisable to mold the ideas into a proposal to conduct the research at other institutions.

Once the research is done and the report drafted, new faculty should solicit critical feedback on their manuscripts from interested practitioners in addition to senior scholars (Boice, 1992). The current system for attaining tenure in most institutions rewards junior faculty more for publications directed toward a restricted audience of higher education scholars than for publications directed toward a broader readership. Although junior faculty members who wish to attain tenure must devote most of their writing time to addressing the scholarly audience, with a little help, they need not wait until tenure to also reach practitioners and stakeholders. Rather than trying to write for practitioners themselves, new faculty might seek assistance from their campus public information office. Public information officers are often experienced journalists and can help faculty reframe their research findings into short, tightly written press releases more likely to be read by administrators, legislative aides, or the general public than the faculty member's own carefully crafted scholarly articles.

Gatekeepers—Reviewers, Editors, and Senior Scholars. Scholars who serve as journal reviewers, editors, and members of tenure review committees make decisions that affect the overall direction of higher education research as well as the career paths of junior faculty. Editors and reviewers play a critical gatekeeping role, according to former *Journal of Higher Education* editor Robert Silverman, who said, "It is not enough that the authors get it right; the field should ask itself how it learns and grows as a field since it is gatekeeper qualities that foster such development" (1993, p. 510). Manuscripts accepted for publication in top higher education journals will not necessarily be simplified if they appeal to both scholars and practitioners. Instead manuscripts might meet two standards: the publications should help practitioners understand higher education in a way that will improve practice, and they should contribute to a theoretically useful body of knowledge (Lawler, 1985). Higher education journal editors might follow the examples of physics and biology journal editors. In their analysis of a stratified random sample of 350 articles from twelve top biology and physics journals, Berkenkotter and Huckin (1995) found a noticeable shift from 1944 to 1989 in the way journals present scientific findings. Specifically, authors are increasingly highlighting statements of their experimental results in titles, abstracts, introductions, and section headings, whereas methods sections are presented in reduced type or in appendixes. This shift, which increasingly accentuates newsworthy information in journal articles, also provides evidence that scientific journals can and do adapt to readers' needs (Berkenkotter and Huckin, 1995). Certainly, editors of higher education journals could raise the standards for applicability and specificity in the *implications for practice* sections of journal articles. Too often, these sections include hastily written platitudes that show minimal understanding of the likely utility or impact of research results on day-to-day practice in colleges and universities. Reviewers could contribute to the development of all scholars by providing suggestions for expanded and truly relevant implications for practice sections.

Senior scholars who mentor and review assistant professors of higher education for promotion and tenure are also gatekeepers whose recommendations ultimately shape the direction of research for the field as a whole. Terenzini asked, "Do we write for publication, and thereby, enhanced prospects for promotion and tenure? Or do we write to make a difference in the lives of others? That is not a dichotomous choice, of course, but the overlap at present is, I suspect, far smaller than it might be" (1996, p. 10). The choice, of course, ultimately rests more with senior faculty, who set standards for tenure and promotion, than with junior faculty, who are striving to meet those standards. Assistant professors' efforts to reduce the research-practice gap can only be tentative until such efforts are strongly supported, if not enacted, by their senior colleagues. "Doing research that makes a difference," according to organizational theorist R. H. Kilmann, "must, therefore, alter the design of research units, the performance criteria that guide their behavior, and the capacity of the system to adapt to the knowledge it creates—to practice what it preaches" (1985, p. 154). Higher education scholars who study faculty work, knowledge systems, and the impact of college experiences on learning seem ideally located to practice what they preach when it comes to fostering the work of junior faculty that advances both practice and theory.

There are several ways that senior scholars might help reduce the research-practice gap when reviewing junior faculty members' portfolios. First, they might review all publications, including lay publications and evaluation reports for practitioners, for their contributions to theory and practice, rather than automatically rating articles published in scholarly journals as somehow better. Senior scholars might give more weight, however, to service that enhances practice rather than service to faculty members' own departments or scholarly community. Finally, as a candidate's portfolio moves up for review at the university level, senior scholars can make a strong case for well-designed and clearly written research that meets two high standards—the improvement of practice as well as the advancement of knowledge.

Practitioners. Administrators, policy analysts, and faculty in other disciplines can do much to enlist new higher education faculty in efforts to improve practice. Higher education faculty can provide service to their university communities in at least two ways. The first involves service on college and university committees similar to that performed by faculty in any and all disciplines. New higher education faculty in particular, however, should be nominated to serve on committees related to their areas of scholarly inquiry. That way, the committees benefit from the assistant professors' background knowledge, and the assistant professors are likely to gain insight and information about current issues facing their own and other higher education communities. Often when campus issues are problematic enough to require more expertise than a faculty committee can provide, administrators hire consultants to conduct research or evaluations. Rather than hiring outside consultants, administrators might allocate funds to hire their local higher education experts to conduct theory-driven research (Chen and Rossi, 1983) that addresses institutional problems. Finally, practitioners can provide collegial feedback on assistant professors' manuscript drafts, paying particular attention to the implications for practice section.

Conclusion

The cost of silence for assistant professors who do not publish at all is very high. "Nonwriters," according to Boice, "have little say in shaping the policies, the funding, and the core educational materials of their disciplines" (1992, p. 161). Writing exclusively for an audience of one's scholarly peers in higher education, however, is another form of silencing. Those who do not write for practitioners are likely to have little say in shaping the policies, the funding, and the core educational materials of the higher education enterprise. New faculty can enhance the depth and applicability of their scholarship by building relationships with administrators and engaging in "the practice of listening as a process aimed at the birth of thinking and interaction" (Fiumara, 1990, p. 149).

References

Augustine, N. R. "Rebuilding Engineering Education." *Chronicle of Higher Education,* May 24, 1996, pp. B1–B2.

Becker, J. S. *Writing for Social Scientists: How to Start and Finish Your Thesis, Book, or Article.* Chicago: University of Chicago Press, 1986.

Berkenkotter, C., and Huckin, T. N. *Genre Knowledge in Disciplinary Communication: Cognition/Culture/Power.* Hillsdale, N.J.: Erlbaum, 1995.

Birnbaum, R. "Policy Scholars Are from Venus: Policy Makers Are from Mars." *Review of Higher Education,* 2000, 23(2), 119–132.

Boice, R. *The New Faculty Member: Supporting and Fostering Professional Development.* San Francisco: Jossey-Bass, 1992.

Bolton, R. "Listening Is More Than Merely Hearing." In J. Stewart (ed.), *Bridges Not Walls.* New York: McGraw-Hill, 1990.

Brown, J. *The Definition of a Profession: The Authority of Metaphor in the History of Intelligence Testing, 1890–1930.* Princeton, N.J.: Princeton University Press, 1992.

Chen, H. T., and Rossi, P. H. "Evaluating with Sense: The Theory-Driven Approach." *Evaluation Review,* 1983, 7(3), 283–302.

Colbeck, C. L. "Merging in a Seamless Blend: How Faculty Integrate Teaching and Research." *Journal of Higher Education,* 1998, 69(6), 647–671.

Conrad, C. F. "Meditations on the Ideology of Inquiry in Higher Education: Exposition, Critique, and Conjecture." *Review of Higher Education,* 1989, 12(3), 199–220.

Creswell, J. W. *Faculty Research Performance*. ASHE-ERIC Higher Education Report No. 4. Washington, D.C.: Association for the Study of Higher Education, 1985.

Dunn, D., Rouse, L., and Seff, M. A. "New Faculty Socialization in the Academic Workplace." In J. C. Smart (ed.) *Higher Education: Handbook of Theory and Research*, Vol. X. New York: Agathon Press, 1994.

Fiumara, G. C. (C. Lambert, trans.). *The Other Side of Language: A Philosophy of Listening*. New York: Routledge, 1990.

Friedson, E. *Professional Powers: A Study of the Institutionalization of Formal Knowledge*. Chicago: University of Chicago Press, 1986.

Goodman, P. S. "Critical Issues in Doing Research That Contributes to Theory and Practice." In E. E. Lawler and Associates (eds.), *Doing Research That Is Useful for Theory and Practice*. San Francisco: Jossey-Bass Publishers, 1985.

Gudykunst, W. B. (3rd ed.). *Bridging Differences: Effective Intergroup Communication*. Thousand Oaks, Calif.: Sage, 1998.

Hackman, J. R. "Doing Research That Makes a Difference." In E. E. Lawler and Associates (eds.), *Doing Research That Is Useful for Theory and Practice*. San Francisco: Jossey-Bass, 1985.

Hearn, J. C. "If Not Us, Who? Thoughts on Policy-Related Work by Higher Education Faculty." Paper presented at the annual meeting of the Association for the Study of Higher Education, Miami, Florida, November 1998.

Kaufer, D. S., and Geisler, C. "Novelty in Academic Writing." *Written Communication,* 1989, 6(3), 386–311.

Keller, G. "Trees Without Fruit: The Problem with Research About Higher Education." *Change,* 1985, 17(1), 7–10.

Kilmann, R. H. "Response and Commentary." In E. E. Lawler and Associates (eds.), *Doing Research That Is Useful for Theory and Practice*. San Francisco: Jossey-Bass, 1985.

Lawler, E. E. "Challenging Traditional Research Assumptions." In E. E. Lawler and Associates (eds.), *Doing Research That Is Useful for Theory and Practice*. San Francisco: Jossey-Bass, 1985.

Lawler, E. E. and Associates (eds.). *Doing Research That Is Useful for Theory and Practice*. San Francisco: Jossey-Bass, 1985.

McColl, G. S., and White, K. D. *Communicating Educational Research Data to General, Nonresearcher Audiences*. Washington, D.C.: ERIC Clearinghouse on Assessment and Evaluation, 1998. (ED 422406 98)

Melander, E. R. "The Man from Mississippi: An Essay on Conversation." Paper presented to the State College Literary Club, University Park, Pennsylvania, May 1999.

Milam, J. H., Jr. "The Presence of Paradigms in the Core Higher Education Journal Literature." *Research in Higher Education,* 1991, 32(6), 651–667.

Miller, D. W. "The Black Hole of Education Research: Why Do Academic Studies Play Such a Minimal Role in Efforts to Improve the Schools?" *Chronicle of Higher Education,* 1999, 45(48), A17–A18.

Mills, C. W. *The Sociological Imagination*. New York: Oxford University Press, 1959.

Peterson, P. L. "Why Do Educational Research? Rethinking Our Roles and Identities, Our Texts and Contexts." *Educational Researcher,* 1998, 27(3), 4–10.

Pettigrew, A. M. "Contextualist Research: A Natural Way to Link Theory and Practice." In E. E. Lawler and Associates (eds.), *Doing Research That Is Useful for Theory and Practice*. San Francisco: Jossey-Bass, 1985.

Silverman, R. J. "The Voice Below 'the Voice': Authors' Reactions to Peer Review." *Review of Higher Education,* 1993, 16(7), 499–512.

Terenzini, P. T. "Rediscovering Roots: Public Policy and Higher Education Research." *Review of Higher Education,* 1996, 20(1), 5–13.

Tierney, W. G., and Bensimon, E. M. *Promotion and Tenure: Community and Socialization in Academe*. Albany: State University of New York Press, 1996.

Townsend B. K., and Weise, M. D. "The Higher Education Doctorate as a Passport to Higher Education Administration." In J. D. Fife and L. F. Goodchild (eds.), *Administration as a Profession*. New Directions for Higher Education, no. 76. San Francisco: Jossey-Bass, 1991.

CAROL L. COLBECK is assistant professor of higher education at the Pennsylvania State University.

4

A learning community made up of all the stakeholders is an effective strategy for moving beyond the research-practice gap. It is enriched by diverse methods and frameworks as well as diverse perspectives and voices. Ways to build such a community include encouraging dialogue between higher education insiders (practitioners) and outsiders (scholars) and transforming the role of journals and professional meetings.

To Be More Useful: Embracing Interdisciplinary Scholarship and Dialogue

Clifton F. Conrad, Ramona Gunter

There is a clear need for scholarship that is more useful for multiple stakeholder groups—policymakers, faculty, administrators, and academic leaders both within and outside higher education—to bridge the gap between scholarship and practice in higher education. Although myriad explanations have been advanced to explain the gap, probably the most widely cited is that it is largely due to an unacceptably narrow definition of what is legitimate scholarly research; namely, that quantitative inquiry is much more rigorous and objective than qualitative inquiry. Indeed more than a few critics of the hegemony enjoyed by quantitative inquiry in higher education research argue that experimental research designs rarely produce useful knowledge because they force one to look for causal relationships within data that have been decontextualized, thereby "causing errors in judgment, and generating utopian proposals because [such research designs assume] that persons are independent, unsocialized actors and not shaped, conditioned creatures as well" (Keller, 1998, p. 269).

In suggesting new directions for higher education research, we begin with two assumptions. One, we take the position that any discussion that holds alternative approaches to inquiry in opposition inhibits the likelihood of research leading to more useful knowledge. As Lindsay and Newmann (1988, p. 34) point out, "Lack of appreciation of the broad scope and diverse orientations to research and the adoption of a narrow definition of 'research' . . . [can] lead to a loss of flexibility, diversity, and vitality in the research activity of universities." Two, we assume that the way in which we frame the challenge is critical both to understanding and addressing the gap between research and practice.

From our perspective, the gap between higher education research and practice is best understood as a failure to provide compelling pictures (as defined here, pictures that resonate with the everyday needs and challenges of practitioners) of the higher education landscape. In effect, the majority of contemporary research offers pictures that are very limited—skewed, truncated, or focused on one level of abstraction or angle of repose to the exclusion of others. An example (including the consequences) of limited pictures and, in turn, the failure to produce useful knowledge—is illustrated in this tale, "A Russian factory worker, it is told, was in the habit of pushing the wheelbarrow through the factory gate at quitting time. Every evening the guards would inspect the wheelbarrow and, finding it empty, let the worker pass. After some months, it was discovered that the worker was stealing wheelbarrows" (Peacock, 1986, p. 11).

The time is right to break through the conventional boundaries that surround disciplinary inquiry, especially boundaries between disciplines, boundaries separating theory and research from practice, and boundaries separating scholars from practitioners. We need to think more holistically and synergistically about what can be done to develop more compelling pictures that directly address the needs and realities of practitioners in the field. We propose in this chapter an interdisciplinary view of scholarship and suggest some strategies for enhancing interdisciplinary dialogue.

The chapter is divided into two parts. In the first part, we discuss our interdisciplinary view of scholarship by urging the acceptance of diverse methods and frameworks and the incorporation of diverse perspectives and voices. To that end, we urge enlarging the membership of our *scholarly community*. In the second part, we propose two strategies—encouraging conversation between and among higher education *outsiders* and *insiders* and rethinking the role of journals and professional meetings—for cultivating and sustaining interdisciplinary dialogue aimed at developing and sharing useful knowledge.

An Interdisciplinary View of Scholarship

Elaborating on our contention that there is a need to develop more compelling pictures for the stakeholders in the field, we emphasize that pictures or models are not statements about what something *is* but rather tools for enriching understanding and informing action. As such, different types of pictures or models can provide different insights into the same subject matter. For example, two different, and apparently contradictory, models—light as particles and light as waves—are used to explain various phenomena related to light.[1] Both models are necessary to explain the behavior of light. In much the same vein, we suggest that various models and frameworks can explain different aspects of what is being studied in higher education. With this definition in mind, we turn to three signature features of our interdisciplinary view of scholarship—diverse methods and frameworks, diverse perspectives and voices, and an enlarged (more diverse) membership in our scholarly community.

Diverse Methods and Frameworks. We begin by encouraging a nonconventional conversation regarding the development of knowledge that recognizes the strengths of diverse methods and frameworks, including cross-disciplinary, intradisciplinary, and interdisciplinary. To be sure, such a plea for greater understanding and appreciation for diverse approaches to inquiry is hardly new. As Boyer puts it, "Research at the boundaries where fields converge . . . is, in fact, increasingly important as traditional disciplinary categories prove confining. . . . Today, more than at any time in recent memory, researchers feel the need to move beyond traditional boundaries, communicate with colleagues in other fields, and discover patterns that connect" (1990, p. 20). Calling for a synthetic approach to the study of human behavior, Clifford Geertz writes, "It is a matter of integrating different types of theories and concepts in such a way that one can formulate meaningful propositions embodying findings now sequestered in separate fields of study" (1973, p. 44). From our perspective, the field of higher education is ideally placed to meet the challenge of developing an interdisciplinary view of scholarship: our subject matter is, by definition, interdisciplinary, and the scholars (including practicing professionals in higher education) who can inform this new conversation are extraordinarily diverse in terms of methods, frameworks, agendas, and perspectives.

If such a view of scholarship is to gain more footing, we must recognize the strengths of various nontraditional ways of knowing that do not have the high status long enjoyed by quantitative methods. Lincoln, in calling for researchers to reemphasize context and the criticality of diversity when explaining findings, notes that many researchers using nonquantitative methods are still operating on the edge of their disciplines—the periphery—and that their work is often not well known. Such researchers are "fighting over the problems of primacy and legitimacy, and they are fighting over access: access to outlets for publication, and fair review of their non-conventional theorizing and research" (Lincoln, 1989, pp. 58–59). Clearly, the faculty reward system in many universities continues to play a pivotal role in slowing the production and accessibility of such nonconventional research. As Fox writes, "By reinforcing standards of success, the reward structure can serve to perpetuate intellectual hegemony and obstruct innovative paradigms that threaten established intellectual traditions. It can function to control junior members of the academy, disguise power struggles, and justify decisions that are, in fact, particularistic" (1985, p. 258).

For many in higher education, rigor in inquiry has been closely associated with quantitative modes of inquiry, even though nontraditional methods have carefully defined standards of rigor. The conventional conception of rigorous analysis is that it is characterized by quantitative findings that support or refute causal statements, and more often than not, these findings are reached only through statistical analysis. Oddly, some proponents of qualitative methods appear to accept the association between rigor and quantitative methods. Lincoln, for example, urges researchers to "[grapple] with inquiries which aim at larger understandings, *even at the expense of some rigor*" (1989, p. 58, emphasis added). We do not believe that qualitative research should be done at the expense of rigor. As Wildavsky writes, "Incorporating new theories, like cultural analysis, and new methods, like social construction, is entirely compatible with the strictest standards of falsification and verification. What is the point, I ask, of trying out new theories and methods if one simultaneously rigs the rules in their favor" (1993, p. xii)?

From our perspective, research—including research based on a philosophy of knowledge that holds that all knowledge is relative, that there are many competing truths, and that complete objectivity is a polite fiction— should not be at the expense of rigor. As Wildavsky argues, "A belief in the importance of subjectivity does not necessarily negate the existence of objectivity, that is, the effort to come to a closer, better, less subjective understanding" (1993, pp. 162–163). In our view, we need to decouple the concept of rigor and the process of quantitative analysis. The processes by which researchers come to "less subjective understandings" is in our view precisely what constitutes rigor. Both quantitative and qualitative data are based on observations and interpretations. If observations are accurate, a data set is complete, and interpretations are grounded in the data, then the resulting analysis can lead to theory and understanding that can and should be subjected to processes of verification and falsification. These processes are fundamental to statistical analysis, and we scarcely need to remind the reader that the value of statistical analysis rests firmly in the quality of both the data and the interpretations. Processes of verification and falsification are no less central to the analysis of qualitative data. This is illustrated in the description by Haworth and Conrad of the process of qualitative analysis that they used in developing a theory of high-quality programs in higher education, "While many of the attributes of high-quality programs we had identified in the first stage were modified and refined . . . others were refuted by negative evidence or insufficiently supported by the data. The remaining attributes were confirmed by the data with little modification. . . . In the third stage of data analysis, we further delimited and tested the theory. . . . In particular, we systematically looked for negative evidence to refute each of the attributes included in the emerging theory" (1997, p. 23).

Rigor is a quality of careful, critical thinking—in both qualitative and quantitative research—that must be employed at every stage of inquiry. All valid and reliable research must employ great rigor in defining the problem, collecting and analyzing the data, and reporting the findings. From our perspective, specious arguments that marginalize nonquantitative methods on the grounds that they undercut rigor should not be given undeserved credence.

Diverse Perspectives and Voices. If the academy were to recognize more fully the value of alternative methods and frameworks, we might merely see the production of more research using nonconventional methods that over time would no longer be nonconventional. But this would not go far enough in creating more compelling pictures of higher education. We envision a more dynamic interaction among scholars about various research findings—an interaction that would include and enlarge Boyer's concepts of the *scholarship of integration* and the *scholarship of application*. Boyer writes, "In proposing the *scholarship of integration,* we underscore the need for scholars who give meaning to isolated facts, putting them in perspective. By integration, we mean making connections across the disciplines, placing the specialties in larger context, illuminating data in a revealing way . . . serious, disciplined work that seeks to interpret, draw together, and bring new insight to bear on original research" (1990, pp. 18–19). Boyer goes on to say, "The *scholarship* [emphasis added] *of application,* as we define it here, is not a one-way street. Indeed, the term itself may be misleading if it suggests that knowledge is first 'discovered' and then 'applied.' The process we have in mind is far more dynamic. New intellectual understandings can arise out of the very act of application—whether in medical diagnosis, serving clients in psychotherapy, shaping public policy, creating an architectural design, or working with the public schools. In activities such as these, theory and practice vitally interact, and one renews the other" (1990, p. 23).

We embrace Boyer's definitions of the scholarship of integration and application, and we also extend the definition of the scholarship of integration by suggesting that it is not solely an autonomous activity done only by those who seek to find new understanding in the research findings of others. *Reflective practitioners* should be encouraged to integrate compelling theories and frameworks into their work no less than full-time researchers of higher education. We also emphasize that the scholarship of application invites a broadened view of practitioners—not merely as instruments for applying theory but also as sources of knowledge and insight through feedback based on their experiences and through their own research as well as researcher-practitioner partnerships.

An Enlarged—More Diverse—Membership in Our Scholarly Community. Interdisciplinary scholarship invites us to embrace an enlarged, more diverse community of scholars: useful knowledge comes from those who can offer different insights and perspectives. Indeed it is our contention that we too often uncritically rig the rules in our favor when we discount information that is not generated by other researchers like ourselves or when we discount the experience of practitioners. In so doing, we insulate our findings from the critiques of others: such insulation prevents our research from being enriched and expanded through the perspectives of others who, given the opportunity, can ask useful questions and provide critical insights that have the potential to move research in new and productive directions. In a nutshell, we propose that we enlarge and diversify our scholarly community to include not only higher education scholars but also scholars in related disciplines and fields of study, and no less important, higher education practitioners.

By way of elaboration, we envision an engaged scholarly community (characterized by the essential component of dialogue) of scholars who have, for the most part, common research interests and goals but who are necessarily diverse along several dimensions. Scholars in such an interactive community should not only be diverse in terms of the methods and frameworks they use but also in terms of their position to the subject matter (whether their perspective is more *emic* or more *etic*, concepts discussed in the following section). Such diversity, we argue, is necessary if their dialogue is to contribute to a richer, more meaningful understanding of higher education. A scholarly community that is homogeneous with respect to methods, frameworks, and position is inherently limited in terms of the observations and experiences that can inform the dialogue within that community and subsequently limited in terms of the meanings that can derive from diverse points of view, making it much like the two-dimensional beings in Abbott's *Flatland*. The experiences of the protagonist of Flatland illustrate how our preferred—and sometimes *only*—ways of understanding guide what we come to view as knowledge and how new information, from a different perspective, can lead to new understanding:

> Imagine a vast sheet of paper on which straight Lines, Triangles, Squares, Pentagons, Hexagons, and other figures, instead of remaining fixed in their places, move freely about, on or in the surface, but without the power of rising above or sinking below it, very much like shadows—only hard and with luminous edges—and you will then have a pretty correct notion of my country and countrymen. Alas, a few years ago, I should have said "my universe": but now my mind has been opened to higher views of things [Abbott, 1952, pp. 3–4].

After the protagonist gives his grandson a lesson in two-dimensional geometry (the only kind of geometry that exists, according to Flatlanders), the grandson raises a disturbing question, which the protagonist relates:

> Upon this, my Grandson . . . took me up rather suddenly and exclaimed, "Well, then, if a Point by moving three inches, makes a Line of three inches represented by 3; and if a straight Line of three inches, moving parallel to itself, makes a Square of three inches every way, represented by 3^2; it must be that a Square of three inches every way, moving somehow parallel to itself (but I don't see how) must make Something else (but I don't see what) of three inches every way—and this must be represented by 3^3";
> "Go to bed," said I, a little ruffled by this interruption: "if you would talk less nonsense, you would remember more sense" [pp. 65–66].

Through a conversation with a sphere that has entered Flatland—a scholarly dialogue, if you will, in which the two strive to understand how their differing perspectives can inform each other—the protagonist begins to develop a modest understanding of the third dimension. During this conversation, the sphere states:

> I am not a plane Figure, but a Solid. You call me a Circle; but in reality I am not a Circle, but an infinite number of Circles, of size varying from a Point to a Circle of thirteen inches in diameter, one placed on the top of the other. When I cut through your plane as I am now doing, I make in your plane a section which you, very rightly, call a Circle. For even a Sphere—which is my proper name in my own country—if he manifest himself at all to an inhabitant of Flatland—must needs manifest himself as a Circle.
>
> Do you not remember—for I, who see all things, discerned last night the phantasmal vision of Lineland written upon your brain—do you not remember, I say, how, when you entered the realm of Lineland, you were compelled to manifest yourself to the King, not as a Square, but as a Line, because that Linear Realm had not Dimensions enough to represent the whole of you, but only a slice or section of you? In precisely the same way, your country of Two Dimensions is not spacious enough to represent me, a being of Three, but can only exhibit a slice or section of me, which is what you call a Circle [p. 73].

We take it that the protagonist began to come to a new understanding only through the experience of surprise upon meeting a circle who could change its diameter or disappear altogether—unheard of in Flatland. "Without surprises, without expectations against which to compare what is happening, we would lose all contact with the world we both live in and change. Surprises—the mistakes we go on and on making—are profound truths, even though (indeed, precisely because) they cannot tell us what is true" (Thompson, Ellis, and Wildavsky, 1990, p. 72). The way in which we use our expectations guides how we deal with new information. Our tendency is to fit new information into our current understandings and when we cannot do so to discard them as anomalous. Because this tendency can profoundly limit the potential of new information to inform us, we encourage scholars to have a more tentative view of their expectations, to see their current understandings as a work in progress, and to welcome the unexpected. As Thompson, Ellis, and Wildavsky write, "Since we usually think it smart to discard our mistakes as untruths, we will have to put ourselves through some unfamiliar intellectual contortions before we can see them in this more favorable light. Instead of throwing them away, we will have to collect our surprises (as if they were precious botanical specimens) and scrutinize them for their similarities" (1990, p. 72).

In short, we encourage scholars of higher education to more consciously seek diverse perspectives, both in their own work and in enlarging our community for purposes of enhancing diversity in perspectives, and in so doing seize surprise at every opportunity. Such a dialogue can be sustained in a community that is open to sharing ideas and inviting critical feedback—a community open to surprise. As Conrad (1989) and others have suggested, a key tenet of a scholarly community—one that is open to surprise—should be that all claims of knowledge are tentative and subject to organized skepticism. In supporting such a tenet, the challenge is to create networks for dialogue that embody organized skepticism, the function of which is to move research (and researchers) in different, better, more productive directions. Although dialogue can take many forms, in the following section we suggest several strategies to facilitate such a dialogue.

Strategies for Enhancing Interdisciplinary Dialogue

In this second part of the chapter, we propose two strategies for promoting interdisciplinary dialogue that can help give expression to the interdisciplinary view of scholarship advanced in the preceding section. The first strategy, which builds directly on the discussion of the need for a broadened definition of our community of higher education scholars, is to encourage conversation between and among outsiders (traditional scholars of higher education) and insiders (practitioners of higher education). The second strategy is to rethink the roles of journals and professional meetings in enhancing interdisciplinary dialogue.

Encourage Discourse Between and Among Outsiders and Insiders. Communication, informal as well as formal, across a diverse community of scholars has great potential to inspire new insights. For example, conversations between researchers who quantitatively describe social phenomena or who explain it through abstract social structures and researchers who provide thick descriptions grounded in the experience of individuals have rich potential. Robust qualitative descriptions may help explain quantitative findings and help bring understanding to the strengths and limitations of the explanatory potential of various models. Rich descriptions based on qualitative data can suggest new research questions for researchers who seek to understand social phenomena through quantitative description or the use of social structures. Likewise, patterns suggested by quantitative descriptions can buttress (or not) findings based in qualitative descriptions and can suggest new research agendas for qualitative researchers.

Less understood and appreciated, in our view, is the value of inviting to the conversation scholars with differing positions with respect to the subject matter. The more embedded in the social environment we are, the more emic our understanding is; that is, the deeper our understanding is of unstated norms and meanings. An etic perspective, by contrast, derives meaning from categories and concepts that are (usually) created by an outsider. The quest for objectivity is central to the reluctance of *outsider researchers* to take into account the emic understandings of the *insider practitioners*. (We should note that insiders are also reluctant to give credence to the outsider perspective.) The more emic our understanding, it is thought, the less objective our observations and interpretations. On the contrary, we assert that objectivity is not inherent to observations of researchers who distance themselves from the phenomena (nor is subjectivity inherent to the observations of the insider). As Harris writes, "It is clearly possible to be objective—i.e., scientific—about either emic or etic phenomena. Similarly, it is equally possible to be subjective about either emic or etic phenomena" (1979, p. 35). Objectivity is not a function of one's position with respect to the subject matter, but rather it is a quality of reflexive practice, wherein the researcher constantly revisits his or her assumptions and scrutinizes the research designs for underlying assumptions that may or may not be valid.

Emic understanding often eludes the outsider. At the same time, the etic perspective—manifested in the categories that outsiders create and the social structures they impose in order to explain phenomena—may or may not prove enlightening to the insider. Too often emic understanding and etic perspective are treated as a dualism, and the resulting differing accounts are viewed as incommensurable. For example, Anderson and Herr discuss a conversation between two researchers regarding their mutual research site (a school) and their findings. At the time of the study, one of the researchers (whose study was based on natural experiments) was employed at the school, and the other was a university-based researcher (whose study was quantitative). Anderson and Herr write:

> The conversation evolved to assessing the school's stated commitment to diversity as discerned through the researchers' differing data sets. Conclusions varied, with Herr convinced that the school's public discourse around issues of equity and diversity "served the purpose of cultivating an aura of progressive change while in actuality maintaining the status quo." For the other researcher, "the jury was still out" and he wondered aloud whether the school, while not being entirely successful, might not be making an honest effort toward change and inclusiveness.
>
> In musing through the conversation later, the questions raised for Herr through the exchange were ones such as: Whose take on the school has more credence? If a university-based researcher draws different conclusions on the setting, whose account will be seen as more trustworthy? Is there room in the research discourse for contradictory accounts of the same setting with both accounts still being seen as "valid" [1999, p. 18]?

We argue that not only is there room in the discourse for contradictory accounts, but they are actually desirable. (Not to diminish concerns about validity, but as Wilfred Trotter states, in science the primary duty of ideas is to be useful and interesting even more than to be true; see Aicken, 1984). The Anderson and Herr account presents an opportunity for both researchers to seize surprise—to engage in a conversation about specific emic understandings that may have eluded one researcher and about specific etic perspectives that may prove enlightening to the other. The goal is to describe how the findings emerged, one informed by emic understanding and the other by etic perspective, and if possible, to explain one set of findings in terms of the other. Although this may not always lead to a different—possibly better—understanding by one or both of the researchers, the potential is there. In *Flatland*, for a fictional example, the sphere was able to explain his etic perspective in terms of the protagonist's emic understanding and to help the protagonist gain "higher views of things."

A particular challenge of higher education research is to understand how emic understandings can inform and advance etic perspectives. Indeed practitioners in the field, who are the most emic of all, often report that their knowledge and experience is discounted. From the field of K–12 education, for example, Delpit documents accounts of minority graduate students in the field of education who attempt to introduce a different, culturally based understanding of children's learning experiences and are systematically referred back to research that disputes their knowledge claims. Delpit provides a poignant example of how informal dialogue among scholars with diverse perspectives—one etic and one emic—can advance the etic perspective. She first describes the etic perspective, one that she came to adopt in graduate school, "I focused energy on 'fluency' and not on 'correctness.' I learned that a focus on 'skills' would stifle my students' writing. . . . I went out into the world as a professor of literacy armed with the very latest, research-based and field-tested teaching methods" (1995, p. 15). She then discusses how her etic perspective was challenged, informed, and changed by a practitioner's sharing of her emic understanding:

> Cathy began talking about the local writing project based, like those in many other areas, on the process approach to writing made popular by the Bay Area Writing Project. She adamantly insisted that it was doing a monumental disservice to black children. I was stunned. I started to defend the program, but then thought better of it, and asked her why she felt so negative about what she had seen.
>
> She had a lot to say. She was particularly adamant about the notion that black children had to learn to be "fluent" in writing—had to feel comfortable about putting pen to paper—before they could be expected to conform to any conventional standards. "These people keep pushing this fluency thing," said Cathy. "What do they think? Our children have no fluency? If they think that, they ought to read some of the rap songs my students write all the time. They might not be writing their school assignments but they sure are writing. Our kids *are* fluent. What they need are the skills that will get them into college. I've got a kid right now—brilliant. But he can't get a score on the SAT that will even get him considered by any halfway decent college. He needs *skills*, not *fluency*.

In puzzling over these issues, it has begun to dawn on me that many of the teachers of black children have their roots in other communities and do not often have the opportunity to hear the full range of their students' voices. I wonder how many of Philadelphia's teachers know that their black students are prolific and "fluent" writers of rap songs. I wonder how many teachers realize the verbal creativity and fluency black kids express every day on the playgrounds of America as they devise new insults, new rope-jumping chants and new cheers. Even if they did hear them, would they relate them to language fluency [Delpit, 1995, pp. 15–17]?

Delpit does not discard this insider knowledge, nor does she try to force it to fit her perspective. Rather she broadens her own understanding by questioning some of the underlying (perhaps previously unidentified) assumptions of her perspective; namely, that teachers, as a whole, have a valid understanding of *all* of their students and that they are able to adequately identify who among their students are "fluent" and who are not. Precisely because emic understandings often elude the outsider (as they are often unstated or invisible), insider knowledge is a crucial contribution to the scholarly dialogue.

Rethink the Role of Journals and Professional Meetings. Publications are the primary venue for the communication of research. Unfortunately—for those who seek an integrated approach to creating knowledge—academic journals generally do not seek practitioner knowledge, nor do they seek to make themselves more accessible to a wider readership (which would include practitioners). As Conrad explains, "Most research by faculty in higher education is oriented to scholarly peers rather than to other stakeholders. . . . The telltale signs are everywhere: specialized books and journal articles that report the results of technical studies; research topics that mirror the interests of [researchers] more than practitioners; the emphasis on quantitative rather than qualitative ways of knowing; and a rhetoric of inquiry that enshrines academic language and a 'stripped-down, cool style' (Firestone, 1987) at the expense of a more public prose" (1989, pp. 200–201).

Because it is our view that scholars will benefit from findings generated by various types of research and from reflective pieces, we argue that journals should play a critical role in sustaining interdisciplinary dialogue. For one, journals can address the overemphasis of quantitative studies by thoughtful inclusion of more qualitative studies. To illustrate, in the field of math and science education research, some qualitative and quantitative studies on student attrition have a symbiotic relationship. Qualitative studies based on the experiences of math and science majors have revealed some social influences that may contribute to students' decisions regarding their majors, and in turn, these studies have provided explanations for the findings of quantitative studies that have described the disproportionate attrition of certain groups from these majors. Such coupling of research findings generated by different methodologies—precisely because in concert, they provide a more compelling portrait—gives readers a greater understanding of the subject matter. Indeed these portraits of student attrition in math and science majors have provided useful knowledge on which student affairs personnel, faculty members, department chairs, college deans, and funding agencies have taken action.

Many practitioners who are engaged in natural experiments and reflexive practices have much to offer, and journals can provide a venue for feedback regarding practitioner experiences. Critical essays, such as Ellsworth's (1989) "Why Doesn't This Feel Empowering? Working Through the Repressive Myths of Critical Pedagogy," offer valuable feedback regarding the adequacy of theory to describe practice. Critical and informed reflections on current theory have the potential to contribute to the refinement of theory. We suggest that such essays should be readily accessible in the same journals that publish the research findings in question. In short, as a strategy for cultivating interdisciplinary dialogue among a diverse scholarly community, scholars should broaden their reading lists. To this end, we encourage journals to diversify. The Eckel, Kezar, and Lieberman chapter (Seven) is an example of a strategy that encourages widespread reading on campus.

Professional-society meetings are yet another potential venue for dialogue. Given the inherent interdisciplinary nature of the field of higher education, distribution lists announcing upcoming conferences and national meetings should necessarily include individuals outside the field of higher education. Conferences, including the Association for the Study of Higher Education and the American Educational Research Association, should call for practitioner papers reflecting on current theory, and conference agendas should include more time and innovative structures for practitioners and researchers to discuss their experiences and findings.

Conclusion

To address the gap between higher education research and practice, we need to provide more compelling pictures—useful knowledge—that directly respond to the challenges and needs of higher education practitioners. We believe that the time is right for embracing an interdisciplinary view of scholarship and introducing new strategies for cultivating interdisciplinary dialogue in order to advance useful knowledge on higher education. Most important, human behavior—the subject matter of higher education research—is infinitely complex. Although the social sciences have greatly contributed to our understanding of human behavior, most scholarly research continues to be unarguably narrow and produces limited portraits. In the words of the (great) sphere, "Your country of Two Dimensions is not spacious enough to represent me, a being of Three, but can only exhibit a slice or section of me, which is what you call a Circle" (Abbott, 1952, p. 73).

Traditional views regarding what counts as knowledge—disciplinary knowledge—and traditional views regarding how knowledge is developed are at
once inadequate and limiting.

To advance useful knowledge in higher education, we have proposed a
more inclusive view, an interdisciplinary view, of our scholarship. The interdisciplinary view welcomes individuals, including higher education practitioners, who can bring differing perspectives and methodologies to bear;
sharpens our understanding of both the strengths and limitations of our theories and findings; helps clarify the contexts in which our scholarship is
meaningful; and whenever possible helps enlarge the context for the integration of scholarship with practice. From our perspective, the view of
interdisciplinarity—with the expanded possibilities of diverse methods and
perspectives, the potential of rich qualitative data as well as quantitative
data, and the synergy of the emic understanding of the insider coupled with
the etic perspective of the outsider—along with the strategies for enhancing interdisciplinary communication advanced here can go a long way to
advancing useful knowledge in higher education.

Note

1. In the eighteenth century, wave theory and particle theory were two competing theories of light. In the nineteenth century, wave theory won out because all observable
phenomena related to light—reflection, refraction, interference, and diffraction, for
example—could be explained with wave theory. But when scientists began to consider
new experiments involving the interaction of light with matter, they found that some of
these interactions could only be understood if they assume that light behaves not as
waves, but as a stream of particles.

References

Abbott, E. A. *Flatland.* New York: Dover, 1952.

Aicken, F. *The Nature of Science.* London: Heinemann, 1984.

Anderson, G. L., and Herr, K. "The New Paradigm Wars: Is There Room for Rigorous
Practitioner Knowledge in Schools and Universities?" *Educational Researcher,* 1999,
28(5), 12–21.

Boyer, E. L. *Scholarship Reconsidered: Priorities of the Professoriate.* Princeton, N.J.:
Carnegie Foundation for the Advancement of Teaching, 1990.

Conrad, C. F. "Meditations on the Ideology of Inquiry in Higher Education: Exposition,
Critique, and Conjecture." *Review of Higher Education,* 1989, 12(3), 199–220.

Delpit, L. *Other People's Children: Cultural Conflict in the Classroom.* New York: New
Press, 1995.

Ellsworth, E. "Why Doesn't This Feel Empowering? Working Through the Repressive
Myths of Critical Pedagogy." *Harvard Education Review,* 1989, 59(3), 90–119.

Firestone, William A. "Meaning in Method: The Rhetoric of Quantitative and Qualitative Research." *Educational Researcher,* 1987, 16, 16–21.

Fox, M. F. "Publication, Performance, and Reward in Science and Scholarship." *Higher
Education: Handbook of Theory and Research,* 1985, I, 255–282.

Geertz, C. *The Interpretation of Cultures.* New York: Basic Books, 1973.

Harris, M. *Cultural Materialism: The Struggle for a Science of Culture.* New York: Vintage Books, 1979.

Haworth, J. G., and Conrad, C. F. *Emblems of Quality in Higher Education: Developing and Sustaining High-Quality Programs.* Needham Heights, Mass.: Allyn & Bacon, 1997.

Keller, G. "Does Higher Education Research Need Revisions?" *Review of Higher Education,* 1998, *21*(3), 267–278.

Lincoln, Y. S. "Trouble in the Land: The Paradigm Revolution in the Academic Disciplines." *Higher Education: Handbook of Theory and Research,* 1989, V, 57–133.

Lindsay, A. W., and Neumann, R. T. *The Challenge for Research in Higher Education: Harmonizing Excellence and Utility.* Washington, D.C.: Clearinghouse on Higher Education, George Washington University, Association for the Study of Higher Education, 1988.

Peacock, J. L. *The Anthropological Lens: Harsh Light, Soft Focus.* Cambridge: Cambridge University Press, 1986.

Thompson, M., Ellis, R., and Wildavsky, A. *Cultural Theory.* Boulder, Colo.: Westview Press, 1990.

Wildavsky, A. *Craftways: On the Organization of Scholarly Work.* New Brunswick, N.J.: Transaction, 1993.

CLIFTON F. CONRAD *is professor of higher education at the University of Wisconsin at Madison.*

RAMONA GUNTER *is a researcher in the Office of Academic Affairs, College of Engineering, at the University of Wisconsin at Madison.*

A new challenge is presented for researchers—being accountable for making their research responsive to practitioners' needs and for helping practitioners learn the importance and application of research results. This new function for the researcher, the teaching-learning function, transforms their role and their relationship to practitioners.

The Educational Role of Researchers

K. Patricia Cross

Is the gap between research and practice analogous to the gap between teaching and learning? Just as there are questions today about whether students are learning what teachers think they are teaching, there are doubts about whether practitioners are using knowledge that researchers think they are providing.

It was assumed, not so very long ago, that the job of teachers was to present knowledge in a clear and organized fashion, and it was the job of students to learn it. In one of the most frequently quoted articles in *Change* in recent years, Barr and Tagg claim that a dramatic shift is under way that makes colleges and teachers accountable for student learning. They write, "A paradigm shift is taking hold in American higher education. In its briefest form, the paradigm that has governed our colleges is this: A college is an institution that exists to provide instruction. Subtly but profoundly we are shifting to a new paradigm: A college is an institution that exists to produce learning" (1995, p. 13).

Is there—or should there be—an analogous paradigm shift in educational research? Is the role of research to provide information or to produce change? Some will argue that the role of the college teacher—or analogously, the role of the educational researcher—is to provide high-quality information. Whether students or practitioners learn or use what is provided is up to them. That position, however, is not persuasive anymore. Many people, including legislators, are holding educational institutions accountable, not just for teaching but also for student learning. Although an occasional ardent defense of research as an activity that exists *to provide knowledge* still appears, it is generally conceded that in applied professional fields such as education, research is an activity that exists *to produce improvement,* if not immediately as a result of the research findings, then certainly in the long run as a result of the knowledge.

The title of the federally funded higher education research center located at Stanford University is the National Center for Postsecondary *Improvement* (emphasis added), and among the explicit criteria for judging the effectiveness of the center is the utility of the research and the degree to which it meets the needs of practitioners. The expectation is clear: federally funded research should result in the improvement of education. Such improvement is most likely to come about not necessarily in the implementation of particular findings, study by study, but rather in the improvement of the knowledge of those who are in a position to make change—largely policymakers and practitioners, including college administrators and faculty. That, I submit, is a teaching-learning function. If research is to lead to improved knowledge, researchers are teachers, and practitioners are learners. (No hierarchy is intended in this statement. The role of researcher as teacher is to facilitate the learning of practitioners in the particular knowledge of the researcher. At times, practitioners will play the role of educators in teaching their specialized knowledge to researchers.) Demands for accountability have raised what we expect from college teachers. Should we raise our expectations for educational research? Certainly we expect it to be responsibly and capably done, and we expect the findings and implications to be made available to practitioners. Should we also expect it to produce change in educational practice?

I will argue that good researchers like good teachers can be held accountable for both the quality of their research *and* their ability to produce change. Unlike many of the critics of educational research, however, I am less concerned about the quality of the research produced than about the ability of the research to produce educational improvement. This is not so much because I think that the quality of the research is unassailable but because I think that the safeguards are more adequate in the area of quality than in the area of accountability for improvement.

The most vigorous criticism of the quality of educational research comes from inside the academy, and that is probably as it should be. One harsh critic of educational research complains that it is "profuse," "picayune," and "often the subject of ridicule" (Keller, 1985, p. 7). Another complains that current research methods "trivialize educational questions into oblivion by reducing data only to what is measurable" (Eisner, 1992, pp. 8–9).

Although there is plenty to criticize in the nature and quality of educational research, I believe that peer review is alive and well in educational research. The research establishment does consider itself accountable for the *quality* of research. Researchers review the work of their peers and are in turn reviewed through juried journals and local, national, and international forums. As critics, researchers are fearless and without peer. They are reasonably articulate, careful, and analytical regarding the work of fellow researchers—albeit never reluctant to state that they would have done it differently, used a different methodology, operated with a different set of empirical assumptions, or followed a different epistemology altogether. There is ample, and in my opinion quite justified, criticism of the overemphasis on positivistic, quantitative studies. And methodology receives near-obsessive review and criticism. Indeed I suspect that peers are more likely to criticize methodology than they are to criticize the topic or question under investigation. We leave it to those external to the educational research establishment to ridicule and belittle the questions for investigation.

The model that has been established for the peer review of research has an enviable record in academe. Indeed advocates for the improvement of college teaching contend that current models for evaluating the scholarship of research might serve as useful models for evaluating the scholarship of teaching. Lee Shulman, president of The Carnegie Foundation for the Advancement of Teaching, writes that if teaching is ever to be regarded as scholarship, "It should be public, susceptible to critical review and evaluation, and accessible for exchange and use by other members of one's scholarly community" (1995, p. 5). Those criteria are in place for the review of research as scholarship. So although much remains to criticize in the quality and questions of educational research, the appropriate review processes appear to be in place. Researchers are judged by their peers as researchers, but their effectiveness as teachers receives little or no attention—despite the fact that unlike classroom teaching, the teaching of their research to practitioners is public, subject to critical review, and accessible for exchange and use by others.

There are interesting parallels between holding institutions of higher education accountable for the learning of their students and holding the educational research community accountable for the improvement of education. Institutions are meeting the demands for accountability for student learning in three ways—by improving the teaching of individual classroom teachers, by recognizing the collective responsibility of the total faculty for the quality of undergraduate education, and by devising appropriate measures of student learning outcomes. It might be instructive to apply these three action steps to the role of researchers as educators.

Educational Role of Individual Researchers

Critics complain that educational researchers cannot, or at least do not, communicate their research so that practitioners learn from it. Researchers, they charge, are not interested in addressing the problems that practitioners must solve nor in cultivating understanding on the part of practitioners, nor are their teaching skills adequate to the task. These are essentially the same criticisms that are prevalent today in the criticisms of classroom teaching to produce learning. They fall into the general concerns about ineffective teaching methods, inadequate teaching skills, and insufficient motivation and rewards.

Ineffective Methods. It is puzzling that researchers have developed knowledge as scholars that they fail to use in practice as educators. Researchers would be the first to caution that lectures and reading assignments are overused in college teaching because they fail to engage learners actively in constructing their own understanding. Yet when it comes to educating practitioners, researchers rely heavily on written reports, lectures, and other methods of dissemination that follow the formula of *teaching as telling.* The problem ought to be painfully clear to researchers: the gap between knowing something and putting it into practice is a chasm that is not easily bridged by dissemination of research results through the traditional channels of lectures and research reports.

One thing we know with a high degree of confidence is that *telling* learner-practitioners what we know is not likely to result in major changes in practice. Learner-practitioners need to be actively engaged in making the knowledge their own. Practitioners seem to recognize this need. There is a growing demand for workshops, collaborative learning groups, and other forms of active learning, and professional associations are requiring more interactive sessions at their conferences. Many conference sessions, however, are superficially interactive, with a few minutes added to the end of the PowerPoint lecture for questions and answers. Questions are random, frequently unheard by many in the audience, and rarely do they build on one another to create a theme or a focused discussion. But the demand is present, and researchers are trying with varying degrees of success to engage learner-practitioners in active learning. The problem is that researchers, like the professors that most of them are, have very little training in conducting productive learning sessions. They lack the skills for effective teaching.

Teaching Skills. What skills does it take to be a good teacher, and can researchers develop those skills? It is not very popular these days to talk about teaching skills. The swinging pendulum now favors language about producing learning. Indeed some people, jumping with a certain amount of irrational exuberance on the learning bandwagon, speak of the need to turn our attention *from* teaching *to* learning. There is, of course, a point to be made, but it takes a skillful teacher to produce learning. And researchers could well give serious attention to the development of teaching skills.

A decade or so ago, it was popular to study the characteristics of good teachers, usually as defined by students. Students rated teachers highly who were enthusiastic, were knowledgeable about their subject matter, showed concern for students, stimulated interest, were available, encouraged discussion, and explained clearly (Abrami, 1985; Feldman, 1976, 1978, 1988). There is nothing especially surprising about that list of desirable characteristics. Moreover, it is probably reasonable to conclude that practitioners would apply pretty much the same characteristics to researchers that they appreciate and are likely to listen to. They would rate highly researchers who know their subject matter, explain clearly without excessive use of jargon and technical phrases, stimulate interest, show concern for practitioners, encourage discussion, and are available. Thus one way to approach the topic of the educational role of researchers is to apply the characteristics of the good-teachers model and implore researchers to observe and develop the characteristics of good teachers. Although some researchers make a real effort to make their work clear and understandable, it is generally conceded that researchers write and speak primarily for the limited audience of fellow researchers.

The most basic of instructional skills includes the requirement that the message must be presented in clear, understandable language free of jargon and appropriate to the backgrounds and interests of the learners. Admittedly, written reports will continue to play an important part in the role of researcher as educator. Yet complaints about research writing continue unabated. Keller (1985, p. 8) claims that "research in higher education is crippled by its expository defects," its "use of jargon and the passive voice, and its lack of literary grace." Well, yes, research writing in education is not going to win any prizes for literary grace. Perhaps we can hope that the attention given to improved writing throughout the school system will eventually appear in the writings of researchers. But certainly graduate schools that train the researchers must demand better writing. All too often, graduate schools ruin a potentially good writer by insisting on passive voice, "scientific objectivity," four-syllable words when simple words will do, third-person references to "this researcher" (when referring to oneself), and other horrors associated with academic writing. It is my impression, not always enhanced by reading the products of professional and research journals, that journal editors are giving increased attention to written exposition, and book publishers tell me that poorly written books do not sell.

Just as written reports will continue to play a role in the learning of practitioners, so too will oral reports at professional conferences, and researchers are showing marked improvement in presentation skills. Although reading papers at professional disciplinary meetings is still done, there is an explosion of visually impressive and audience-friendly techniques in evidence at most conferences these days. PowerPoint and other presentation enhancements are common, and graphs, outlines, and even cartoons enliven presentations. But aids such as PowerPoint have also contributed to the demise of thoughtful lectures that engage the audience intellectually. Too many presenters use visual aids as a public outline—and little more. They simply read their outline of notes from the screen to the audience. Sound teaching theory would commend the use of both visual and auditory channels to convey information, yet the intellectual challenge that would engage the audience in active thinking is replaced by a mundane presentation of information.

Good teachers possess a wide variety of teaching methods and skills. Their artistry comes in selecting the method appropriate to the situation. Some research information, such as figures and tables, is probably still best presented in print or in simple overheads. A provocative, challenging lecture that engages the audience is still in style, despite prevailing criticism of teaching as telling. Small-group interactions are effective when there is adequate time and space and the task assigned is appropriate to audience needs and experience. In sum, many researchers are presenting their information well, and a few are truly great teachers, their passion and engagement with their subject matter an inspiration to learners everywhere; but it may be time for some new models of researchers as educators.

We have created an artificial gap between researchers and practitioners by assuming that researchers address universal issues whereas practitioners address local problems. In truth, if research is going to improve practice, it must be applied locally. Moreover, local issues are repeated hundreds of times at campuses all across the country. Right now, almost every campus wants to know how to assess student learning, whether learning communities really work, how to improve student writing skills, how to restructure a reward system to recognize good teaching, and a host of other issues that are universal across higher education.

Judith Ramaley proposes in Chapter Six the creation of an institutional studies office on campus, where researchers give particular attention to helping administrators interpret and apply national research findings locally. I would go further and suggest that campuses might establish one or more learning communities consisting of researchers and administrators who sit down together on a regular basis to learn from one another what issues need study, whether relevant research already exists and if so how it can be applied to the local situation, and how the campus can be involved in ensuring continued scholarly inquiry into its own effectiveness. The learning community would follow the known principles of small-group learning; that is, participants contribute their particular knowledge and skills in a way that makes them *interdependent* in solving a problem or addressing an issue. This is a quite different model from practitioners telling researchers what needs to be studied and researchers telling administrators what is already known through research.

A learning community consisting of researchers and practitioners on a single campus has certain undeniable pragmatic virtues, which are mentioned by Ramaley, but it also has a persuasive cognitive rationale. Learning from diversity is widely supported for students, albeit too often narrowly associated primarily with race and ethnicity. The cognitive virtue of diversity is its requirement to view something from another's perspective. Rather than assuming that the human mind is a logical machine that inevitably reaches truth through rational procedures alone, we take the viewpoint of the other, and it reminds us that every interpretation is embedded in a particular situation. Practitioners see issues differently from researchers, and the diversity of perspectives should enrich the learning of both. In the past, researchers have felt virtuous if they consulted practitioners about the problems to be studied; this is a different proposal. It requires practitioner and researcher to see the issue from the perspective of the other and to operate interdependently in analysis and problem solution.

A problem with the proposal for local researcher-practitioner learning communities is that rewards for practitioners are local, whereas the rewards for researchers are usually national and international. Is there an appropriate reward for researchers who participate in local learning communities? **Motivation and Rewards.** Problem solving seems to be an intrinsically rewarding activity for human beings. Therefore one could contend that working together on a local problem could be one of the most intrinsically rewarding activities of academic life. Extrinsic rewards may be a different matter. Historically, university-based research centers funded by external sources have had a fear of being co-opted by their administrations to work on local problems; as a result, the common practice has been to distance themselves from administrators and "their" problems.

I am going to argue, however, that the rewards for researchers as educators can and should operate quite effectively, in both traditional and nontraditional ways. In the traditional reward structure, the question is, Is there a national and international market for research on local problems that rewards the scholarship of the research? Can researchers working on local problems gain disciplinary recognition? In a less traditional mode, the question might be, How can institutions reward scholars working collaboratively with practitioners in learning communities on their own campuses?

In general, the personal reward for scholarship is national recognition and tenure. National recognition brings mobility and offers from other institutions. Tenure, at present, is heavily dependent on national recognition, but it is locally granted. There is no obvious reason why an outstanding professor-researcher should not be granted tenure for scholarship that is recognized by his or her local faculty colleagues as contributing to the improvement of learning on that campus. Can a so-called local researcher get published and gain recognition from disciplinary colleagues? I believe that the answer is a clear yes. I believe that there is both a need *and* a ready market for the kind of work that could be generated by researchers working in the context of learning communities on educational issues. Who would not be interested in the scholarship and research generated by a local learning community consisting of a psychologist, anthropologist, ethnic studies specialist, student affairs administrator, and academic affairs officer? Or how about a learning community that included an economist, business management professor, demographer, and academic and business affairs administrators? The combinations of academic and administrative talents that could be put together are endless, and it is highly likely that the research emerging from such collaborative efforts would be of great interest to national and international audiences as well as to local constituents.

In sum, rewards for addressing educational issues through research on local issues do exist, but they are not currently exploited. If a campus makes a unified commitment to recognize and reward researchers who conduct good scholarship on educational matters of concern to the campus, there is no good reason why rewards—extrinsic as well as intrinsic—should not be forthcoming.

Educational Accountability of the Research Community

So far, I have addressed the adequacy of teaching methods, skills, and rewards for individual researchers, but a larger question concerns the responsibility of the research community for the improvement of educational practice. Two examples will illustrate some encouraging efforts to make research useful to practitioners. One is the trend toward integrating and synthesizing research studies across a broad array of disciplines and topics to derive some general principles for *good practices*. The other is the trend toward developing *exemplary models* that can be used as ready-to-adapt improvements. Both are designed to reduce the work of practitioners in translating the findings of research into applications, and they have been at least moderately successful in getting the attention of practitioners. Although they represent a start toward assuming a collective responsibility for improving the practice of education through research, both have problems when it comes to applying the best that we know about how people learn.

Integrating and Synthesizing Research. Educational research has been criticized because it is not cumulative; instead of building a temple of knowledge brick by brick, social scientists tend to scatter ever more bricks around the brickyard. In recent years, however, there has been a determined effort to gather the bricks together to build on past research. Meta-analysis has become a respected and valued method within the research community for integrating the findings of hundreds of separate studies into at least a tentative conclusion about what we think we know about a given topic. The next level of integration is illustrated by the prodigious efforts of some researchers to synthesize the state of knowledge in higher education in large books covering almost every realm of practice. Feldman and Newcomb (1969) performed this service in 1969 for the significant research that had been done in higher education during the previous forty years. In 1991, Pascarella and Terenzini (1991) performed a similar service, reviewing over twenty-six hundred studies relevant to higher education. These tomes are too large, too detailed, and too focused on the precision of research language to be very useful to practitioners, hence the appearance of the super-condensed, bulleted lists of *principles of good practice.*

In 1987, a group of researchers with special dedication to the application of research to practice gathered at Wingspread with the daunting assignment of synthesizing the research on student learning over the previous fifty years into easily understood principles for good practice. The result, probably the most widely distributed list of research findings in the history of higher education, is known as the *seven principles for good practice in undergraduate education* (Chickering and Gamson, 1991). The success of this list of bulleted practices has spawned a generation of highly condensed, easily digested sound bites freely distributed to a wide variety of practitioners. (See, for example, American Association for Higher Education, American College Personnel Association, National Association of Student Personnel Administrators, 1998; Angelo, 1993; Education Commission of the States, 1996; McCombs, 1992; Oxford Centre for Staff Development, 1992.) Such lists represent a step in the right direction in three respects: they communicate with practitioners in a language that is easily understood; they integrate research across disciplines and projects; and they assume a collective responsibility for the responsible uses of research to improve practice. Used well, the bulleted principles serve as a highly useful starting point for discussion. Used poorly, they can circumvent learning for deeper understanding by grasping at a quick and too simple conclusion to be implemented whenever and however possible. Consider an example.

The first principle of good practices is that good practice encourages student-faculty contact (Chickering and Gamson, 1987). Researchers know that much lies behind that conclusion, most of it in the climate and attitudes that exist on a campus where student-faculty contact is prevalent. But practitioners looking for a quick fix may interpret the finding quite literally and implement the research by funding faculty meals in the dormitories, for example. That may be a good thing to do, and it may provide the impetus for growing a healthy campus climate; but by itself, it is not likely to produce the greater student satisfaction, retention, and learning that seems implied by the research. A good discussion of the many factors that lie behind this finding is probably more likely to result in honest change than is a quick program for funding, but the realities of practice operate poorly in such a trade-off. Administrators can implement on their own the funding of faculty meals with students. Convening groups of faculty members to discuss the creation of a campus climate for meaningful student-faculty contact is an altogether different matter.

What responsibility does the research community have for deeper learning, that is, for creating an understanding of what lies behind the bulleted principles? Some dedicated researchers would say that it raises a new question for investigation: Does faculty discussion of the principle result in more meaningful change than administrative funding of an implementation? That is not only a tough question to investigate—and quite possibly not worth the effort—but also an abdication of the role of meaningful learning in favor of empirical evidence. Empirical evidence inevitably comes in bits and pieces, and it is hard to put it all together without the glue of common sense. Just as the primary responsibility of good teachers is to connect bits of isolated information into meaningful relationships that form an understanding of the discipline, so the responsibility of researcher-educators should be to create an understanding of the meaning behind research findings. Cognitive scientists would be pretty disdainful of teachers who pulled together the major premises of their discipline into a neat set of principles that encapsulated the research of the past fifty years and distributed it to their students! So although the seven principles, and the numerous progeny they have spawned in every aspect of educational research, have been a significant advance, they should not be considered a final answer in fulfilling the role of researchers as educators. They are very useful as the *starting point* for discussion; they are incomplete as conclusions to be implemented.

Exemplary Models. A second approach to the problem of putting the knowledge generated by research into practice is the development of exemplary models. The initial development of an exemplary model applies the very best of what we know about learning: it requires critical analysis; is problem based, collaborative, and active; involves frequent assessment and feedback; is situation-based; and is actively self-monitored. Understandably, it is often a rich learning experience for those actively involved in developing the model. Creators of the exemplary model may take pride in their achievement to the point of becoming stars in the educational firmament, with enviably heavy calendars for travel and speaking engagements; but their audiences are often just that—audiences. Active learning to solve a problem that has high relevance for the developers of the model becomes a passive learning experience for those told about it.

The problem with the exemplary model is that its adoption by others is frequently disappointing, and it is expensive when the *exemplary practice* fails to spread beyond funded projects. Given some concerted attention and adequate funding, research projects could be designed to build in good teaching practices from the beginning by involving consortia of practitioners who work as teams to solve a problem. To their credit, funding agencies are beginning to involve consortia in translating research into practice. But operating consortia is a complicated teaching-learning business on campus and off. On campus, it requires working teams coming together from different parts of the campus to solve an institutional problem—or to improve the institution's accountability for the learning of its students. Off campus, operating an effective consortium requires interinstitutional teamwork to apply a common knowledge base to campuses with different climates and histories. The challenge is not unlike teaching to the different personalities and learning backgrounds that populate college classrooms today, but the very diversity of different viewpoints and perspectives may be of as much value to the scholarship of applied research as it is to the learning of students.

Accountability Measures for Educational Research

Just as student outcomes measures are being devised to help colleges and universities fulfill their obligation to produce learning, so too should measures be devised to ensure the accountability of research to produce improvement. The objections to this proposal will be familiar, especially to researchers who have been in the forefront of helping institutions devise measures of student learning. They include complaints that improvements in learning (or educational practice) occur over a long period of time, are multifaceted and too complex to be measured, depend on the situation (mission) and intent, and other similar arguments against making the effort to measure outcomes. Granted, the student learning outcomes that have been devised to aid institutional improvement and ensure accountability are far from perfect, but the serious search for measures of accomplishment has stimulated an awareness and purposefulness that was not present when it was simply assumed that colleges were producing learning. Through experience and many false starts, the assessment movement has moved away from externally imposed measures of achievement toward institutionally devised measures that show institutions (and external constituents) how well they are accomplishing their purposes. Although it is common for funding agencies to request a plan for dissemination in the proposal, there has been little insistence that dissemination efforts be specifically designed to produce improved practice beyond the funded project; nor has there been the kind of follow-up that we are seeing in the assessment movement. If the purpose of educational research is to produce improvement, should not the educational community insist on evidence? (If the purpose of the research is not to improve practice, then researchers should, of course, be encouraged to state what the purpose is and how we will know whether they have achieved it.) Evidence is a familiar and revered term to researchers, yet there is precious little evidence collected and disseminated by researchers to demonstrate that they are making a difference in educational practice. Higher education has been accused for generations of wanting to reform everyone except itself—of resisting the look in the mirror that would tell it how it is doing. Is it time for researchers to look in the mirror?

References

Abrami, P. C. "Dimensions of Effective College Instruction." *Review of Higher Education*, 1985, 8(3), 211–228.

American Association for Higher Education, American College Personnel Association, National Association of Student Personnel Administrators. *Powerful Partnerships: A Shared Responsibility for Learning*. Washington, D.C.: American Association for Higher Education, American College Personnel Association, National Association of Student Personnel Administrators, 1998.

Angelo, T. A. "A 'Teacher's Dozen': Fourteen General, Research-Based Principles for Improving Higher Learning in Our Classrooms." *American Association for Higher Education Bulletin*, Apr. 1993, pp. 3–7, 13.

Barr, R. B., and Tagg, J. "From Teaching to Learning: A New Paradigm for Undergraduate Education." *Change*, 1995, 27(6), 13–25.

Chickering, A. W., and Gamson, Z. F. (eds.). *Applying the Seven Principles for Good Practice in Undergraduate Education*. New Directions for Teaching and Learning, no. 47. San Francisco: Jossey-Bass, 1991.

Education Commission of the States. "What Research Says About Improving Undergraduate Education." *American Association for Higher Education Bulletin*, 1996, 48, 5–8.

Eisner, E. "Are All Causal Claims Positivistic?" *Educational Researcher*, 1992, 22, 8–9.

Feldman, K. A. "The Superior College Teacher from the Students' View." *Research in Higher Education*, 1976, 5, 43–88.

Feldman, K. A. "Course Characteristics and College Students' Ratings of Their Teachers and Courses: What We Know and What We Don't." *Research in Higher Education*, 1978, *9*, 199–242.

Feldman, K. A. "Effective College Teaching from the Students' and Faculties' Views: Matched or Mismatched Priorities?" *Research in Higher Education*, 1988, *28*, 291–344.

Feldman, K. A., and Newcomb, T. M. *The Impact of College on Students*. San Francisco: Jossey-Bass, 1969.

Keller, G. "Trees Without Fruit: The Problem with Research About Higher Education." *Change*, 1985, *17*(1), 7–10.

McCombs, B. L. *Learner-Centered Psychological Principles: Guidelines for School Redesign and Reform*. (rev. ed.). Washington, D.C.: American Psychological Association Task Force on Psychology in Education, 1992.

Oxford Centre for Staff Development. *Improving Student Learning*. Oxford, England: Oxford Brookes University, 1992. (Reprinted in "Deep Learning, Surface Learning." American Association for Higher Education Bulletin, 1993, *45*(8),10–11.)

Pascarella, E. T., and Terenzini, P. T. *How College Affects Students*. San Francisco: Jossey-Bass, 1991.

Shulman, L. "The Pedagogical Colloquium: Three Models." *American Association for Higher Education Bulletin*, 1995, *47*(9), 6–9.

K. PATRICIA CROSS *is professor emerita from the University of California at Berkeley.*

6

Achieving transformational change is a scholarly challenge best dealt with by practicing public scholarship, which is modeled by the leader and encouraged in other members of the campus community. Like all good scholarly work, good decision making by campus leadership begins with a base of scholarly knowledge generated and validated by higher education researchers.

Change as a Scholarly Act: Higher Education Research Transfer to Practice

Judith A. Ramaley

In *Educating the Reflective Practitioner*, Donald Schön (1987) says, "In the varied topography of professional practice, there is a high, hard ground overlooking a swamp. On the hard ground, manageable problems lend themselves to solution through the application of research-based theory and techniques. In the swampy lowlands, messy, confusing problems defy technical solutions" (p. 1). As a president, I spend most of my time in the swampy lowlands. When I ascend to the cooler and breezier heights, I find problems that are easier to define and easier to resolve, but less important.

Identifying Problems

A number of years ago, a group of community activists in the Portland metropolitan area in Oregon developed a simple matrix of three types of problems that present themselves to policymakers and community leaders. Real-world problems can be divided fairly effectively into these three types on the basis of the relative degree of clarity of both the questions posed and the solutions offered.[1]

Type one problems can be articulated clearly, and the solution can be chosen from among one or more already well-researched options or remedies. They represent the high, hard ground.

Type two problems can be articulated clearly, but the solution or resolution is not readily apparent, and there are no well-researched choices to consider. Here the ground is getting slippery, but not yet swampy.

Type three problems are confusing difficult-to-characterize "policy messes" for which there is no agreement on either the most important issues or the most promising remedies. These problems often are made more complex by the conflicting values and perspectives of the various stakeholders. Here we are in the swampy lowlands.

Like the reflective practitioner in Schön's text, I frequently encounter unique cases—type three problems—for which no precedent has prepared me, situations in which several significant and sometimes equally important values clash. These are cases that have too many variables, most of them problematic in several ways at once. Schön (1987, p. 4) calls these issues an "ill-defined melange of topographical, financial, economic, environmental and political factors," often, in my experience, changing shape even as they come into focus.

A Learner Among Learners

A decade ago, when I was preparing a keynote address on the subject of the president-practitioner for the Association for the Study of Higher Education (ASHE) meeting in Portland, Oregon, I received a letter from my undergraduate alma mater, Swarthmore College, which was at that time looking for a new president. The college sought a person with these characteristics:

- Strong academic credentials
- Leadership skills
- Strong interest in fostering a culturally and racially diverse community
- High energy tempered with patience, persistence, a sense of humor, and a tolerance for diversity of opinion
- Ability to be visible and accessible and to welcome interaction with other people

What that ambitious portrait and many like it today are missing is a critical point: an administrator today must also be a *learner among learners,* willing to embrace the novel and unexpected and able to be an agent for change. To do this, we presidents must model what it means to have a truly educated mind and then use this mind in public. We must constantly study our environment and test various ideas, let us call them hypotheses, in the living laboratory over which we preside. It would be wise for us to apply to ourselves the same expectations that we have of any well-educated person, whose capacity to think through problems in the swampy lowlands will depend both on the attitudes and knowledge and the skill and experience to employ a rigorous scholarly approach.

There are two interesting and helpful ways to think about scholarship and how we can use a scholarly approach to create a coherent and visionary context for leadership and change. One way to approach being a *public learner* is to practice and model for others what Harry Payne (1996) of Williams College calls the *intellectual virtues,* "the willingness to explore widely, the ability to test one's ideas against those of others, the capacity to listen thoughtfully, the strength to adduce reasons for assertions" (p. 18). Payne traced the relationship between these intellectual virtues and the character virtues of "honesty, humility, integrity, and independence" (p. 18) and made the case that "all learning is for the sake of something beyond the act of learning itself" (p. 18). In this case, the purpose of learning is to support the kind of decision making that can lead to institutional transformation. I have found that one of the things that helps encourage a more scholarly approach to the management of institutional change is to involve my own senior leadership team in the same kind of intellectual inquiry that I would apply to any other challenging scholarly work. My goal is to "learn our way" into an understanding of institutional change. In my experience, learning is a means for institutional leadership to create a meaningful context for transformational change.

In many of the conversations about change in higher education that I have heard in the past several years, the importance of modeling a scholarly approach to leadership was never mentioned. In a world composed primarily of type three (swampy) problems, the act of leadership must become an *act of public learning,* guided by the same expectations that we hold when evaluating any other form of scholarship. Presidents and other administrators must consistently demonstrate a devotion to rigorous inquiry that allows for informed decisions to be made within a *culture of evidence* compatible with the scholarly values that are a defining feature of academic institutions.[2]

The second way to think about the scholarship of change is to use the approach articulated by Ernest Boyer (1990) and then extended by Charles Glassick, Mary Taylor Huber, and Gene Maeroff (1997). For Boyer, scholarship encompassed four kinds of intellectual work—discovery, integration into a body of knowledge, the scholarship of teaching (interpretation), and application. It soon became clear that members of the academy would not accept this broader definition of scholarly work unless the rigor and value of the work could be documented and assessed and its impact properly understood. In the case of a scholarly approach to change, the impact takes shape in large, tangible institutional terms.

Although Boyer died before he could complete this essential phase of the work, Glassick and colleagues (1997) prepared a companion monograph that outlined the features that characterize excellent scholarship, regardless of who conducts the work and where it is performed. These same elements should characterize the work of presidents and senior administrators as well. Rigorous scholarship, as well as good decision making, is characterized by clear goals, adequate preparation, appropriate methods, significant results, effective presentation, reflective critique, and ethical practice and respect for those involved or potentially affected by the work.[3]

As a scholar, a president must think of each day as a glorious experiment and must constantly encourage others at the institution to view every program or case or problem as a learning opportunity, as a vehicle to test basic assumptions about the institution, and as a potential avenue for positive institutional change. Only when the presidential role is approached in this manner can the leader be a public learner and properly lead a genuine learning organization (Senge, 1990; Garvin 1995). At the same time, the call to be a public learner and to model the adoption of a habit of experimentation and the acceptance of the associated risk that accompanies the uncertainty of experimentation can make both the leader and his or her associates anxious. After all, in most organizational environments, the leader is supposed to be in charge, and a leader should not need to ask questions or show the uncertainty that a scholarly attitude will reveal. According to Napier and Sanaghan (1999), "Curriculums [sic] and administrative practices alike have suffered from divided loyalties and narrow frames of reference that make coordination and coherence in direction difficult to achieve" (p. 19). In a university, the values, attitudes and behaviors that should be modeled and encouraged are those of a rigorous scholar, but the approach must be multidisciplinary.

It is uncommon for academic leaders to approach their responsibilities in a scholarly mode. One reason for this is that we do not, as faculty members, usually learn "in public." We prefer to conduct our investigations on our own terms, with conditions set by our own protocols and interests. Then we share our best work with our peers using forms of communication adopted to fit the norms and expectations of our particular discipline. As Napier and Sanaghan (1999) have written, "Most leaders arise within the context of their profession with its clear leadership traditions and particular beliefs." To this insight, I would add that we also learn and then share what we know according to particular rules and norms.

A challenge faced by any institutional leader who wishes to view institutional change as a *scholarly act* is that the research base on issues in higher education that might support a scholarly approach to academic leadership is spread across many different fields, built on a variety of different methodologies, and reported in a variety of different communication styles and technical vocabularies—qualitative and quantitative, individual observations as well as comparative studies, theoretical and practical. The interdisciplinarity of the research base that might guide good decision making in a university setting represents a significant barrier to its use. It is difficult for a practitioner to find the relevant studies and reports, to validate their contents, and to assess the degree to which a particular set of findings might be generalized to the administrator's own institution and circumstances.

Ways to Encourage Public Learning in Others

A university is a special form of democracy that seeks to provide an environment where all persons can do their best work and develop as educated human beings, whatever role they play within the organization—student, faculty, staff, administrator, trustee, or advisory board member. To accomplish these goals, everyone must continue to learn, and change itself must be both an intentional and a scholarly act. To accomplish this consistency of behavior, the president must model and encourage public learning. Although many strategies might support the infusion of the experimental mode into the governance and administration of a university, four approaches, taken together, have proven very effective.

First, it is important for a leader to instill a discipline of reflection and a culture of evidence, insisting that everyone back up their opinions and observations with real information, not just perceptions. I frequently ask, "How do you know that?" when faced with a critic who claims to be in possession of the truth. To my delight, the self-appointed critic rarely has any objective evidence for his or her criticisms or alarming observations.

Second, it is essential to create new patterns of conversation that encourage and support the involvement of everyone in defining the issues that will be important in building the organization. There are many ways to do this. As I prepare this chapter, my own institution is engaged in a strategic change initiative. In the first stage, the senior campus leadership learned new approaches to problem solving. We also experimented with new ways to involve a broad-based segment of the campus community in defining questions critical to our future and in identifying and then evaluating strategies that we might employ to address our critical issues.

As the process unfolds, a record is being kept on the University of Vermont home page for anyone to examine and follow over time. There you can see the schedule of activities, the results from each stage, and the logic behind the process as a whole. Reports will also appear in our campus faculty-staff newspaper. In this model, three new forms of conversation and communication are being used to ensure campuswide accessibility to the process—carefully designed interactions that promote careful listening and thoughtful, informed input to the process; use of a Web site to provide a map to the overall change process and a record of the results obtained at each stage; and regular open forums and interactions to allow people to ask questions and satisfy their concerns about what is happening and what it might mean.

A third component of an experimental or scholarly mode is to adopt a philosophy of experimentation and the active management of reasonable risks. Several universities have begun to replace the more traditional concepts of risk and risk management with a broader domain of risk bounded by legal, financial, public relations, and institutional integrity considerations. This new philosophy, which actively promotes the management of known risks and a more experimental approach to the generation of campus strategies, results in the establishment of some of the features of a learning organization.

Presidents, like everyone else, operate within the norms and methodologies of their home disciplines. As a scientist, for example, I have explicit assumptions about how to frame a question, how to test the validity of hypotheses I have about the issue, and how to communicate my results or findings to others. Given my own scholarly background, I react more quickly and favorably when someone else communicates their concerns or findings in a "scientific mode." My provost, who is a social scientist, has quite different intellectual habits from my own. This complementarity of disciplinary perspectives is helpful on a senior leadership team, especially during a time of intense change. As Peter Senge (1990) has written, "The organizations that will truly excel in the future will be the organizations that discover how to tap people's commitment and capacity to learn" (p. 4). Transformational change itself also depends on superior learning (Eckel, Green, and Mallon, 1999).

The final and fourth strategy needed to establish a successful learning enterprise is to create new ways to facilitate access to information, so that everyone can make informed choices.[4] In many institutions, essential information such as budget details appear mysterious. A number of institutions, including my own, are moving to the use of benchmarking and *dashboard indicators* to measure critically important aspects of institutional performance. These measures are readily available and are frequently posted on a Web site.

In a college or university undergoing meaningful and intentional change, a leader can serve as the facilitator of a research team by building a shared vision for the future, challenging unexamined assumptions and bringing to the surface mental frameworks or models that inappropriately shape everyone's thinking about the issues, fostering more connected learning (Belenky, Clinchy, Goldberger, and Tarule, 1997) and a consideration of the context of individual decisions and choices, and modeling the intellectual virtues and adopting a scholarly approach to change (modified from Senge, 1990).

The State of the Research

Having laid upon the shoulders of presidents and other academic leaders a mantle of scholarship, we are faced with two key questions: What body of knowledge might we consult in order to perform the necessary step of adequate preparation? How can a president acquire sufficient knowledge of the relevant literature and the scholarly work that might illuminate our swampy problems? In 1990, I asked a member of the Institutional Research and Planning Office at Portland State University to tally the topics and themes covered in six national journals and the programs of three national meetings. The journals were the *Journal of Higher Education,* the *Review of Higher Education, Research in Higher Education,* the ASHE-ERIC *Research Report Series, New Directions for Higher Education,* and *New Directions for Institutional Research.* The meetings were the Association for Institutional Research, the Association for the Study of Higher Education, and the Society of College and University Planning—all for the years 1988, 1989, and 1990. The ten

most frequently mentioned topics across all nine outlets for higher education research were (1) institutional governance-management-organization,
(2) planning, (3) assessment-outcomes, (4) technology issues and applications, (5a) facilities management, (5b) institutional finances, (6a) faculty
salaries-personnel issues, (6b) the role of institutional research, (7) student
success-achievement, (8) admissions and enrollment, (9) community colleges, and (10) student issues-conduct.[5]

In a second study, the University of Kansas Office of Institutional
Research and Planning studied the tables of contents of *Change*, the *Journal
of Higher Education, Research in Higher Education*, and the *Review of Higher
Education* over the period from January 1988 through June 1990. The
themes were sorted out by using the ERIC search descriptions for each article. The results were interesting. The most popular topic in all four journals
was college faculty. After that, the themes diverged. The list of topics
included minority and gender issues on campus, college students, educational change, the conduct of research, leadership issues, and the presidency.

Although many of these topics sounded interesting, they were not of
particular use to me in 1990 as I struggled with a steep learning curve as a
new president. I dragged home a foot high stack of "homework" every
night, consisting of correspondence, copies of other people's letters, materials from various higher education associations, articles that someone had
copied and thought I should read, and reports from campus groups. In the
case of the campus reports, the authors had taken months to prepare the
documents and were nonetheless expecting an answer from me within a day
or two. As a scientist unfamiliar with qualitative research methods and the
scholarly approaches used by social scientists, I did not know how to assess
the validity of most of these studies and reports, nor could I determine their
usefulness to me as a practitioner. In addition, they did not match up very
well with the list of the top ten issues that I was thinking about in those
days as a new president. At that time, in the fall of my first year, I had the
following issues on my mind:

1. *Women and minorities.* There were only five articles on diversity, thir-
    teen on minority students, and twelve on women in academia, a total
    of less than 10 percent of the articles on planning and institutional gov-
    ernance.
2. *University-industry partnerships and technology transfer.* These were not
    on the list at all.
3. *Fundraising.* There were only eleven articles or speeches on this topic.
4. *Team building and professional growth of staff.* These issues were not vis-
    ible as such but possibly contained as a section within some of the
    many leadership articles, most of which I did not have time to read.
5. *Community college and high school articulation.* There were only thirty-
    one articles and presentations on these topics (in sharp contrast to the
    interest that at least K–12 articulation elicits today).

6. *College athletics.* There were only six articles and presentations.
7. *Research centers and institutes and interdisciplinary work.* There were eight articles on these topics.
8. *Conflict resolution and good decision making.* There were none.
9. *Enrollment management and fostering student success.* There were thirty-three articles.
10. *Effective on-campus and off-campus communication methods.* There probably were none unless they were buried inside another topic.

As I write this chapter in 1999, I am two years into my second presidency at the University of Vermont. Perhaps partly as a factor of my greater presidential experience and partly because I now serve a different kind of institution in changing circumstances, my list is actually now much longer than the one I constructed in 1990. I had some difficulty deciding which items to put in the top ten. In addition, my problem list now appears in the form of questions rather than themes. Unable to confine myself to a simple ten items, I expanded the list to a baker's dozen. Even so, many of my key questions did not make it onto the list:

1. Does investment in research really lead to the creation of jobs and to economic development? How can I make the case that investing in my university is truly an investment in the state's future? What are the best ways for universities to participate in economic and community development?
2. How can my institution best participate in the rapidly growing information age and the increasingly complex knowledge marketplace? What is intellectual property now? How will the knowledge media develop and who will prepare materials for these media?
3. Is there a path toward a sustainable fiscal future? How can I reconcile the competing demands of affordability and access on the one hand with the demands to spend ever increasing amounts for academic excellence, increasing health care costs, technology, and competitive compensation for faculty and staff on the other?
4. Are there meaningful differences in the way students learn, what they learn, and how much they learn in classroom and community settings where they have direct contact with one another and with faculty when compared with distance learning and various forms of *virtual* experiences? How much should we invest in the capacity to do distance learning, and what form should our participation take?
5. What strategies can I use to promote more effective communication within the campus community, with the trustees, and with our external constituencies? What can I do to get across important messages and information in the flood of information that crosses everyone's desk and computer screen every day?
6. What does academic quality really mean, and how can I measure it?

7. How can I truly involve members of the campus community meaningfully in setting the direction of the institution and obtain buy-in for the agenda we are developing? What does it really take to initiate and sustain meaningful institutional change?

8. What are the best ways to contain and then decrease problem drinking among our students? How can we best collaborate with the community to deal with the shared consequences of drinking among high school and college age youth?

9. How can we create truly multicultural competency and a climate that supports diversity on campus, and by the way, how would I know that we had done so? How can we detect and then effectively deal with bias incidents and promote harmony on campus?

10. What can we do to ensure a successful and meaningful student experience and live up to our aspiration to prepare our students to live creative, productive, and responsible lives?

11. How will work be done in the university of the future, and how should we classify jobs to reflect the changing nature of work?

12. What forms will effective governance (decision making) take in the university of the future, and how can we ensure meaningful participation of trustees, faculty, staff, alumni, and students in defining and addressing the institution-shaping issues that we will face over the next decade?

13. By what means can we learn together fast enough to keep up with all of these issues? What does it take to produce a true learning organization?

With the assistance of a doctoral student, Mika Nash-Gibney, I reviewed the major topics contained in the same set of journals in 1998–1999. This review yielded a long list of topics, here presented as a baker's dozen. The topics were as follows—(1) approaches to K–16 reform and the importance of school-university partnerships; (2) the use of technology and distance learning; (3) governance; (4) curricular design and the meaning and purpose of an undergraduate education; (5) university-industry collaborations; (6) national educational policy issues; (7) multiculturalism, affirmative action, and admissions standards; (8) service learning; (9) nontraditional students and adult learners; (10) workforce preparation, competency-based testing, and needs of employers; (11) reform of the lending process-regulatory burdens and direct lending; (12) national ranking schemes and higher education quality and standards; and (13) tuition discounting, cost containment, and institutionally based aid. Although many of these topics would be helpful to policymakers, they do not appear on the list of many of the presidents I know. I would hope in the future for more overlap between institutional concerns like mine and the research interests of higher education researchers.

In 1990, most of the things I was worrying about did not show up in the higher education literature at all. I did find my concerns in other publications aimed at presidents or trustees or administrators, but these articles were not based on any scholarly research. They were usually in the form of essays and opinion pieces, sometimes supported by methodologies and observations that I might apply to my own circumstances but usually based on broad assumptions and assertions that were not held up to close scrutiny or tested.

In 1999, the list of research topics in the higher education literature looks very different from the pattern a mere decade ago, indicating that researchers are paying much closer attention to the major issues faced by higher education. Some of my issues and questions still do not show up in the scholarly literature, although they are regularly addressed in publications such as *Change* or monographs issued by associations such as the American Council on Education, the Association of Governing Boards, and the American Association for Higher Education. Most of these reports are reflections on experience, but they frequently lack the rigor of scholarly analysis and assessment, leaving me unsure what validity to assign to these pieces. A few of my concerns have not shown up very often, if at all, in the typical parade of publications that comes across my desk (for example, issues 6, 11, and 13 from my 1999 baker's dozen list of issues that concern me), except in the forms of *calls to action* and recommendations for how I should exercise my duty as a president to respond to a particular challenge, such as college drinking or the lack of civility and civic responsibility on college campuses today.

I asked myself in 1990, and I continue to ask myself now, why higher education researchers are not analyzing issues that are most meaningful to people who are faced with the challenge of leading institutions out of the swamp. Where is the base of scholarly knowledge that I could draw on to guide my institution onto higher ground? Why are my colleagues writing personal pieces about issues that I care about but that lack the rigor of scholarly work? Why is it so hard to apply the results of many of the more scholarly pieces to my own circumstances? Above all, why is the field of higher education research so out of sync with the needs of people like me, who are trying to exemplify in our practice of the presidency the same rigorous standards that apply to any other form of scholarly work? Even if higher education researchers *were* publishing exactly what I need, how would I find time or develop the expertise to read the studies and interpret them?

My educated, but untested, answer to all but the last of these questions is that as in most other fields, the faculty who work in higher education are seeking legitimacy within the intellectual hierarchy of the contemporary disciplines. The more that faculty in higher education programs seek status, the more they are likely to pull away from contact with the real world from which they originally drew their questions and in which their findings might be tested in the context of practice. This seems especially paradoxical in the field of higher education because the object of the research in this discipline is the actual world of the institution that lies just beyond the researcher's office door.

When I submitted my manuscript to the editors of this volume, they offered another explanation for the gap between my interests as a chief executive and the content of the scholarly literature on higher education. They pointed out that researchers write for many audiences, including legislatures, students, and parents. I must admit that I doubt that much of this work actually gets into the hands of legislators, students, or parents unless it is translated from the scholarly literature by someone else. However, I would be interested to know more about how researchers who are interested in higher education select their topics for research and who they think the audiences will be for their findings and interpretations.

By trying to dress up any field that derives directly from the practical necessities of a profession, we risk losing the vitality that makes the life of a scholar-practitioner so interesting. My scholarly interests as a president are very much shaped by the realities of the institution I serve and by my external constituencies. In addition, I must be aware of the larger, more general realities of the academic community as a whole, as well as the particular experiences of the community of educational institutions of which we are a part—in our case, the cohort of public research and land-grant universities. The interests of a generalist like me must inherently be interdisciplinary, and I am forced, by the nature of my work, to keep the big picture in mind and to concentrate on the things that matter the most. I cannot worry only about the issues I wish to define, because the world presents me with issues on its own terms, not mine, and with its own urgencies. I cannot use exclusively the language or jargon of any one field lest my faculty and administrative colleagues give me up for lost.

Improving the Scholarly Base

What can be done to create the scholarly base to support the intellectual and knowledge needs of a learner among learners, a scholar-president? As higher education researchers plan their agenda for the future, I hope they will keep in mind some of the needs of presidents and other academic leaders and approach their work with the swampy questions of higher education in mind. It would help if, in selecting topics for investigation, researchers would emphasize issues of interest to policymakers, focus on the big picture, avoid studying small questions, encompass more comparative studies so that a particular institutional experience could be studied in a larger context, and provide a clear interpretation that would allow practitioners to see how broadly the results might be applied to other similar circumstances.

What about my last question? Even if higher education researchers *were* publishing exactly what I need, how would I find time or develop the expertise to read the studies, interpret them, and apply them to the issues facing my own institution?[6] I propose changing the role of the institutional research office, so that it can support leadership and change as an act of scholarship. In most cases, these offices evolved to collect data and provide statistical reports for various compliance reviews. These tasks require the services of data managers rather than scholars (Barbara Holland, personal correspondence with author, June 17, 1999). Institutional research offices should evolve into *institutional studies offices*. These new offices would be staffed by higher education researchers who would help presidents and other academic leaders find and properly interpret the base of existing literature that could be applied to practice. They could also conduct research designed to support transformational change as well as contribute to a shared body of literature on higher education.

The institutional studies office could also be developed as a research center that would support and extend the scholarly work of faculty whose primary appointments are in the academic units, and it could identify and support promising lines of scholarly inquiry that could benefit professional practice and the exercise of leadership. It is common practice for some faculty to hold administrative appointments as directors and chairs of departments and programs. Why not consider an institutional studies appointment or fellowship that would be comparable? A true institutional studies office could help presidents and other academic leaders by serving an R&D function for the institution and its leaders, while at the same time providing technical assistance to faculty members and advanced students who wish to conduct research on issues in higher education. The following are some of the tasks it could perform:

- Evaluate the effectiveness of the new programs we are trying to put in place and assist in creating a base of evidence to support regular program review of continuing programs
- Interpret national data and research by relating them to our own institution, pointing out where the national trends fit our situation and where they do not, and why
- Sort through the case studies, project reports, and monographs that cross my desk in waves and tell me which have application to us, which address issues that we are also facing, and what conclusions the authors have drawn
- Identify people who are doing interesting research on higher education to bring to our campus as consultant-evaluators and to give us an opportunity to reflect on our mission, our progress, and our aspirations
- Do studies that could help us address our own issues more thoughtfully and with a richer base of knowledge about ourselves, our experience, and the relevance of the work of others to our own efforts
- Provide technical assistance to other units on campus that wished to conduct studies of performance or to assess and address issues specific to that part of the institution
- Conduct research that would support the development of new measures of performance to address those elements of our mission that are not

commonly assessed, such as the impact of our community involvement and professional service on quality of life in the community

There is much to be gained from good communication among researchers, managers and administrators, and campus leadership. Good contact can keep all three groups honest. An appropriate bridge builder is the scholar-president, the learner among learners who must slog back and forth between the swamp and the dry highlands. Over the years, I have learned that a frequent shift of perspective between inductive and deductive reasoning, theory and practice, and formal inquiry and application can enrich our scholarship. It is also a useful route to making informed choices that have institution-wide consequences. If researchers always take the high road and presidents and others mostly have to take the low road, "We'll ne'er meet again," to quote the old Scots ballad. If we travel together, we can spin out some fine tales and like the Canterbury pilgrims can entertain one another along the way, while keeping our aspirations and our spirits high.

Notes

1. As far as I know, the ideas were never published, so I use them here without being able to provide a citation.
2. The term *culture of evidence* was used regularly by Steve Weiner, formerly the executive director of the Western Association of Schools and Colleges, to describe the growing importance of assessment and accountability in the design of quality assurance in the institutional review process conducted by regional accrediting bodies.
3. This last element was not presented in Glassick and others as a feature of excellent scholarship, but integrity was mentioned as one of the qualities of a scholar.
4. The four strategies suggested here are based in part on a list found on a large piece of newsprint in the St. Johnsbury Extension Office of the University of Vermont. I was told that it first appeared in someone's church bulletin.
5. 5a and 5b and 6a and 6b indicate that these items were tied for that position on the list.
6. In a few instances, I know that what I want simply is not available, even if I had time to look for it. We really know very little, for example, about adolescent drinking and how best to treat or manage drinking at that age. This knowledge is needed if we are to address the growing problem of binge drinking on college campuses.

References

Belenky, M. F., Clinchy, R. M., Goldberger, N. R., and Tarule, J. M. *Women's Ways of Knowing.* (10th anniversary ed.). New York: Basic Books, 1997.

Boyer, E. L. *Scholarship Reconsidered: Priorities of the Professoriate.* Princeton, N.J.: Carnegie Foundation for the Advancement of Teaching, 1990.

Eckel, P., Hill B., Green, M., and Mallon, R. *On Change: Reports from the Road: Insights on Institutional Change.* Washington, D.C.: American Council on Education, 1999.

Garvin, D. A. "Barriers and Gateways to Learning." In C. R. Christensen, D. A. Garvin, and A. Sweet. (eds.), *Education for Judgment: The Artistry of Discussion Leadership.* Boston: Harvard Business School Press, 1995.

Glassick, C. E., Huber, M. T., and Maeroff, G. I. *Scholarship Assessed: Evaluation of the Professoriate.* San Francisco: Jossey-Bass, 1997.

Napier, R., and Sanaghan, P. "The Changing Nature of Leadership: Implications for Business Officers." *NACUBO Business Officer*, 1999, 33(1), 48–60.

Payne, H. C. "Can Or Should a College Teach Virtue?" *Liberal Education*, 1996, 82(4), 18–25.

Schön, D. A. *Educating the Reflective Practitioner.* San Francisco, Jossey-Bass, 1987.

Senge, P. M. *The Fifth Discipline: The Art and Practice of the Learning Organization.* New York: Doubleday, 1990.

JUDITH A. RAMALEY *is president of the University of Vermont.*

7

Institutional reading groups are vehicles for engaging practitioners in the fast-growing body of higher education literature and for encouraging a culture of information for decision making. These groups are an effective strategy for assimilating large amounts of complex information, fostering new knowledge, and sparking campuswide conversation on important issues.

Toward Better-Informed Decisions: Reading Groups as a Campus Tool

Peter Eckel, Adrianna Kezar, Devorah Lieberman

The challenges that campus leaders face are daunting. Many academic leaders not only are trying to be innovative with fewer resources and to respond more quickly, surely, and strongly to changing demands but also are confronting issues that have become extremely complex. For example, improving teaching is no longer accomplished by simply introducing new texts or developing a new syllabus. The challenge now includes technology, along with its Listservs and chat rooms, the Internet, and asynchronous learning; new research on the brain and learning from cognitive, behavioral, and neurological sciences; and alternative pedagogies, which include service learning, self-taught modules, peer education, cluster courses, and learning communities.

Institutional leaders continually require new tools and new knowledge to adequately address the challenges that are shaping the future of colleges and universities, suggesting that well-prepared leaders will master the ability to draw on current scholarship and writing to stay informed, to think differently about managing their institutions, and to make better-educated decisions. How many of us are prepared to talk about asynchronous learning, developing learning communities, or rethinking lectures based on new brain research? How many can make important decisions deeply informed by knowledge about all three? New insights gained *collectively* from the literature and their intentional application to institutional change make for sound leadership and informed decision making. This chapter explores one strategy, focused reading groups, for helping institutional leaders stay abreast of information and use it to make educated decisions. Reading groups are one strategy for confronting the challenges of too much information coupled with too little time, which Ramaley outlines in Chapter Six. Whereas she proposes a formal, structural change—creating offices of institutional studies (as opposed to more traditional offices of institutional research)—this chapter offers solutions that easily fit within the strengths, values, and structures of most colleges and universities (Eckel, Hill, Green, and Mallon, 1998).

Challenges of Leadership

Among the numerous issues confronting higher education are the burgeoning financial pressures, expanding technologies, changing faculty roles and employment arrangements, new and alternative pedagogies, intensified public scrutiny, changing demographics with diverse learning needs, stronger calls for assessment and accountability, and threatening new competitors (including for-profit institutions). None of these challenges are simple, nor are the solutions likely to be in current academic leaders' repertoires. Many of the most pressing challenges that leaders face cannot be addressed through their current know-how or with routine solutions; rather they require adaptive work (Heifetz, 1995), and in many cases the questions, as well as the answers, are unclear.

At the same time, the amount of information available for academic leaders is overwhelming, and getting larger, deepened by the Internet (Guskin, 1996; Harrington, 1996). Surveys and studies posted on Web sites are now easily obtainable; literature reviews related to literally thousands of topics can be found through the Association for Institutional Research, the Educational Resources Information Center (ERIC), and other Web-based databases. Institutions, state and federal agencies, organizations, and researchers are no longer constrained by the cost and burdens of publication; the information is on the Web. Academic leaders face the challenge of managing growing information while coping with an environment that expects them to use it. The public demands greater accountability in campus decision making (Banta and others, 1996); and many new academic management techniques, particularly strategic planning and total quality management, are grounded in a thorough collection of data and information (Rudolph and Howard, 1996). Leaders are simply expected to know more and to know how to find and use the needed information.

These changes require higher education leaders to develop strategies for keeping current and staying informed. In order to be effective leaders in complex and challenging times, higher education leaders should be well versed in the literature and research for higher education and know how to use that information wisely. This chapter describes one promising strategy for bringing together campus constituents to manage the needed knowledge—reading groups. Repeated concerns suggest there is simply no way to keep pace with today's changes and their demanding new knowledge (Keating and others, 1996; Kezar, forthcoming), yet experience shows that this strategy has proven effective.

Campus Reading Groups: A Proposed Solution

Many colleges and universities are initiating reading groups, or professional seminars as they are frequently referred to, the goal of which is to explore a topic in-depth and provide campuses with a common language and knowledge base about a particular issue, such as faculty workload, community service learning, or campus learning communities. Creating a campus reading group is an intentional strategy for managing the breadth of information, mastering important knowledge, and involving key people. Reading groups build on highly developed academic strengths, such as inquiry, focused thought, writing, and contemplation, to advance institutional goals. They structure learning opportunities for people who favor exploration yet spend much of their time teaching.

The structure of readings groups varies. They may vary by size. One type consists of a cross-campus committee of fifteen to twenty-five faculty and administrators; another type consists of a large percentage of the campus, who read common materials before a retreat. They may vary by the number of meetings. A strategic committee may meet over the course of the academic year. A retreat may occur only once. They may also differ by facilitator. One structure may use a designated facilitator, from inside or outside the institution, to organize, lead, and summarize the conversations and insights. The facilitator role also may rotate among reading group participants, allowing everyone to lead at least one discussion. Finally, reading groups may differ in the use of reading assignments. A common set of papers may be read by all participants; or a reading list may be divided among participants who then summarize, synthesize, and share what they have read. The first design provides a more in-depth analysis of the readings, whereas the second allows for more material to be surveyed.

Reading groups provide an opportunity for many people to gain familiarity with the literature. They are important not only for the immediate information that they give readers but also for creating a *process* for bringing people together for focused discussion and inquiry, which itself is important. Reading groups focus collective attention; highlight specific elements in ambiguous contexts; bring people together who otherwise might not interact, let alone problem solve; uncover institutional assumptions, perspectives, priorities, and biases; and make people aware of differing interpretations of events (Bensimon and Neumann, 1993; Birnbaum, 1988; Schein, 1993). They educate on many levels.

Many of the institutions participating in the American Council on Education (ACE) Project on Leadership and Institutional Transformation, a five-year effort to help twenty-six institutions accomplish ambitious institutional change agendas, used reading groups as an effective change strategy. Campus reading groups are effective strategies for jump-starting and maintaining campus conversations about pressing and complex issues. They are an important tool for exploring *why* an institution must change and for determining a course of action. Conversations help refine ideas and make them more sensible. As a result of the participants continually engaging in informed dialogue, ideas become crystallized and concepts clarified, assumptions are explored and tested, and offensive ideas are rethought and new arguments (defenses) articulated. Those new to the conversation ask probing questions, challenge assumptions, and offer new ways of seeing and perceiving.

Challenges of Using Reading Groups

If reading groups are a straightforward mechanisms for informing decision making, why is it that more institutional leaders are not drawing on the literature in a systematic way? A study of practitioners and their use of the higher education literature asked that question. The study, conducted by the ERIC Clearinghouse on Higher Education, the main collection and dissemination point for higher education literature, sought to identify strategies that practitioners had developed for addressing the issue of effectively utilizing literature for decision making. ERIC staff conducted focus groups at national conferences of people who might use the higher education literature, including department chairs and deans, institutional researchers, student affairs officers, and midlevel administrators from academic affairs and alumni affairs and development. Their findings suggested some of the challenges to developing campus reading groups.

Reasons for not using the literature. The findings suggest that most practitioners do not make decisions informed by the literature, although they acknowledge they should or would like to use the literature to guide decision making. The focus group results suggest that campus leaders did not refer to the literature because it takes valuable time and was perceived to be of little value and to be inaccessible. Potential users also had little institutional incentive to read (even bringing information to meetings often was discouraged) and frequently lacked an understanding of what information the literature contained, and they were overwhelmed by its magnitude. This quotation from one participant epitomizes common reactions, "I know this sounds horrible, but I have stacks of materials and I never refer to it. There isn't even just one reason it sits there, but so many. The people I work for do not value the effort; that is the biggest disincentive. But mostly it is time, I just can never even get the time to think about how I could use the information. Then as it grows, I feel like I will never wrap my arms around it."

Little understanding of the available literature. A second finding was that people were not familiar with the relevant literature that could inform institutional decision making. As issues change or emerge, potential users do not know which newsletters or journals might assist them with exploring the current topic. Many believed the higher education literature was vast, and they did not know what it contained. When potentially useful literature from outside higher education, such as business and management, psychology, or sociology, is added to the mix, the problem becomes even more overwhelming.

Lack of strategies to become familiar. Finally, within an interdisciplinary professional field, such as college and university administration or teaching and learning, the challenge of identifying, sifting, and synthesizing is complex. Focus group participants did not have strategies for effectively reviewing the pertinent information or for quickly distinguishing between high-quality and low-quality literature. One participant offered reading groups as a way to organize administrators to review potentially useful literature. He made this comment:

> We need to use the higher education literature to frame the work that we do, but to be honest there is lots of literature, and it is hard to have the time to determine what is good and worth reading. Especially since we pull in literature from business and management, sociology, public policy, as well as higher education. An institutional reading group that shares important references and resources would cut down on each individual's work. Our institution has begun what we call a collective read. Everyone is assigned different literature sources to review and summarize and to let others know about important pieces that everyone within the institution should read or know about. I think if more institutions did this, then there would be more use of the valuable resources out there.

Formats of Reading Groups

The ERIC study and the ACE project suggest several structures for reading groups that vary around the three design elements presented previously. As with most things in higher education, one size does not fit all, as institutional culture, norms, and expectations will dictate what works and what does not. The following discussion gives several examples of strategies for mastering key literature and engaging faculty, administrators, staff, students, and others in informed decision making. The examples illustrate some of the strategies that were used by institutions in the ACE project.

Focused dialogues. Focused dialogues are group discussions of ten to thirty individuals taken from a cross section of campus life. A set of common readings focuses the conversation. Faculty and administrators are typically included. Depending on the campus culture and norms and on the topic, students, board members, and alumni may also be invited. Participants are asked to speak and listen as citizens of the campus community, not as representatives from particular groups. Focused dialogues are led by a facilitator, who frames questions that arise from the readings, helps summarize major points from the discussion, pushes those involved to think more deeply and build on one another's ideas, and avoids conversational dead ends. For example, leaders at Valencia Community College in Florida engaged their campus in widespread discussion through a series of twelve focused dialogues in which nearly three hundred faculty and staff participated to help shape and make progress on their change initiative,

Collaborating to Become a More Learning-Centered Institution. All of the comments from these dialogues were compiled and circulated collegewide, and all faculty and staff were asked to comment.

Retreats. Retreats facilitate conversations among a broad range of people. Typically spread out over a weekend and held off campus, retreats provide time away from daily worries to concentrate on larger issues. Retreats are useful opportunities for reading groups. Selected articles spur discussion and provide new language and ideas for launching either a new change initiative or revitalizing a current initiative. Retreats may follow a range of formats, from highly structured agendas with a set reading list to nearly open ones that are created as an initial task of the participants, who bring along their favorite readings. Retreats provide valuable and rare opportunities for people to get to know one another in a relaxed atmosphere and build trust and personal relationships that help them work together when back on campus. The University of Puerto Rico in Rio Piedras held two weekend retreats at strategic points in their change process. The retreats were structured to give their faculty and administrators extended time and comfort to do their work.

Seminars. Seminars are regularly scheduled discussions that may focus on a specific issue. Structured much like a graduate-level seminar, they provide a forum for participants to read and discuss a common reading list. The readings frame the curriculum for the seminar. Participants (or teams of participants) may produce a series of discussion papers that come out of the seminar readings. These papers are distributed for the purpose of getting responses from other seminar participants or from the campus community. Because such seminars are scholarly processes, they draw on the participants' sophisticated skills and strengths, allow participants to explore new questions in familiar ways, and lend intellectual substance to institutional decision making. Seminars can take place over an intensive weekend or can be spread out over the semester, much like a course. They can be offered to groups of various sizes; for example, only to the change team, or they can be conducted in sections and open to the entire campus community.

Symposia. Symposia are campuswide conversations that typically include a prominent speaker or speakers, materials written by the presenter, and some type of facilitated conversations. The speakers and their writings, which are disseminated ahead of time, provoke ideas and catalyze thinking; the follow-up conversations allow participants to further explore ideas and implications. Frequently, papers written by the speaker are included with the invitation as a way to spark interest. These conversations may be held in a plenary or may be broken into smaller groups. Symposia may last a few hours or all day, depending on the purpose, the time available, and the speakers. Leaders at Stephen F. Austin University in Texas sponsored three campuswide symposia related to their change agenda. Each symposium featured a nationally prominent speaker to address the faculty. Following the speech, organizers held small-group conversations to discuss ideas provoked by the speaker. Summaries of the forums were posted on the institution's Web site to continue the dialogue on an electronic posting page.

Town meetings. By design, town meetings are open. The entire community is provided with a set of common readings and is invited to participate in a broad discussion to move the institution as a whole to a new level of understanding and consensus. Olivet College in Michigan held a campuswide town meeting to craft their Campus Compact, a guiding statement for the college related to their institutional change initiative, Education for Individual and Social Responsibility. The daylong meeting, held in the gymnasium, involved students, faculty, staff, and trustees (250 people in all) to further define the institutional vision related to the change initiative and to formulate a set of principles about what it means to be a responsible member of the college community.

Reading Groups at Portland State University

One of the institutions in the ACE project, Portland State University (PSU), used reading groups as a cornerstone of their change efforts. Fifteen faculty and administrators initially organized a reading group to provide an intellectual framework for the institution's change agenda, Developing Faculty for the Urban University of the Twenty-First Century. For the first year, the provost facilitated monthly conversations and assigned articles and books that led the group toward a common vocabulary and an understanding of higher education and the changing roles of faculty in an urban land-grant institution.

At the end of the first year of readings and conversations, the reading group identified five themes that it believed the institution needed to address—technology and faculty development, a new definition of scholarship, faculty involvement in curricular management and structure, the effectiveness of the compartmentalized faculty and support roles and structures, and factors that would enhance community at PSU. The reading group formed subgroups for each theme and identified a new set of questions. Each subgroup in turn identified readings related to the subtheme questions and then recruited other faculty and administrators to read and participate in second-generation reading groups. The original group members facilitated these second-generation conversations, which were summarized and posted on the PSU Web site. These became the foundation of the upcoming fall symposium attended by all PSU faculty.

Third-generation reading groups. Many of the texts for the first two reading groups have been incorporated into an expanded third-generation reading group. Led by the provost, faculty and staff signed up to participate in the yearlong series, which met every three weeks for two hours to discuss issues confronting higher education today. Thirty faculty and staff committed to participate in this series, although close to eighty expressed interest. The series will be repeated again this year for a new cohort of thirty faculty and staff. Due to the number of requests for repeat sessions, the institution is also videotaping the sessions, so that all who wish to be part of the learning may do so.

The reading group structure forced PSU faculty and administrators to meet regularly and explore complex concepts together. The meetings provided a scholarly forum to discuss issues that were not necessarily related to any one member's personal agenda, and the readings provided a context in which to struggle with issues related to the changes at PSU. Colleagues began to listen to one another more. A respect formed among group members that carried throughout the project and beyond.

Campus contributions and challenges. Beyond educating faculty and administrators about higher education and placing PSU's challenges in a broader context, the reading groups made campus contributions. First, many of the suggested outcomes from the reading groups influenced the activities of PSU's Center for Academic Excellence (CAE). For instance, five members of the original reading group became part of CAE's board in the center's inaugural year. Second, reading group conversations shaped the fall's Focus on Faculty Day, a one-day event welcoming new faculty and staff that engages campus faculty in a conversation about important campus issues. Third, articles produced by reading group members were published in the *Faculty Focus*, a CAE publication about teaching and learning issues. The groundwork for many of the articles was laid in reading group conversations.

Reading groups also created some challenges. For example, group participants have multiple responsibilities in a variety of contexts across campus. Taking the time to stop and participate in the reading groups was a constant challenge. At times, members expressed concern that they did not have the time or energy to participate to the extent they would like. The provost acknowledged this challenge and asked members of the group to read as much as they could and be present at the meetings as often as possible. This ground rule served the group well. Feelings of guilt for not completing all readings were at a minimum, and the group progressed at a reasonable pace, given individuals' competing demands.

Principles of Reading Groups

The ERIC study and the experiences of the twenty-six institutions participating in the ACE project illustrate the challenges associated with running effective reading groups and offer some solutions. Common challenges include inadequate time, lack of institutional incentives, and limited understanding of available resources in the literature.

To cope with the constraints of time and competing priorities, reading group leaders at PSU gave participants permission to do only as much as they could. No penalties were exacted if group participants did not finish all of the reading. At the same time, it was discovered that reading groups might actually *save* time because participants will learn valuable information that translates into increased performance, and the group can collectively cover more intellectual ground than a single person can. The perception can easily exist that reading groups absorb time, but when a long-term perspective is adopted, reading groups create efficiencies by involving more people who can share the demands of reading and learning.

Another major barrier identified through the focus groups was a lack of institutional incentives. Some strategies for addressing this issue include providing partial release time for facilitators; using reading group participation as a way to meet service requirements for tenure, promotion, or merit pay; and making sure committee chairs reinforce the importance of informed decision making.

Helping reading group members gain an understanding of the breadth of literature and easing feelings of being overwhelmed are easily addressed. The ERIC Web site provides an organizing mechanism for literature (http://www.eriche.org). Reading groups can use available search tools, such as the ERIC database and tutorials, and synthesis documents, such as bibliographies, trend analyses, and digests, to get a handle on the vast literature. The ERIC Web site also has a section called Primer of the Higher Education Literature, which outlines the literature and what types of information are available and how to obtain it.

Several other challenges may emerge, such as dealing with strong ideological disagreement, lack of engagement, and difficulty sustaining the group momentum. Many of these issues are addressed in the literature on small-group work and learning (Johnson, Johnson, and Smith, 1991). Individuals endeavoring to create reading groups should visit a few primers on small-group work as the way to overcome many of these challenges.

Conclusion

This chapter proposes a solution that is not new, simply underutilized. We have taken the well-worn concepts of reflection and intellectual engagement and have proposed structures to institutionalize them to benefit the college or university. Reading groups are efficient structures for highlighting and exploring important topics and for coping with the seemingly endless literature on higher education. They are opportunities to put into practice ideas found in the literature and thereby close the gap. They generate engagement with institutional issues and help individuals who are focused solely within their units see the big institutional picture. Reading groups also help generate commitment to institutional issues. As people become more engaged with related literature, they may become more active in applying new knowledge and challenging current institutional paradigms.

This chapter offers practical solutions for moving beyond the gap between theory and practice. Reading groups can generate new knowledge and a more engaged faculty, and they can catalyze widespread conversations.

These can be strong influences on a campus. Reading groups are one effective strategy for leading today's colleges and universities.

References

Banta, T. W., and others. "Performance Funding Comes of Age in Tennessee." *Journal of Higher Education,* 1996, *67*(1), 23–45.

Bensimon, E. M., and Neumann, A. *Redesigning Collegiate Leadership: Teams and Teamwork in Higher Education.* Baltimore, Md.: Johns Hopkins University Press, 1993.

Birnbaum, R. *How Colleges Work: The Cybernetics of Academic Organization and Leadership.* San Francisco: Jossey-Bass, 1988.

Eckel, P., Hill, B., Green, M., and Mallon, B. *En Route to Transformation.* On Change: An Occasional Paper Series, No. 1. Washington D.C.: American Council on Education, 1998.

Guskin, A. E. "Facing the Future: The Change Process in Restructuring Universities." *Change,* 1996, *28*(4), 26–37.

Harrington, C. F., and others. "Does Institutional Research Really Contribute to Institutional Effectiveness? Perceptions of Institutional Research Effectiveness As Held by College and University Presidents." Paper presented at the annual forum of the Association for Institutional Research, May 1996.

Heifetz, R. A. *Leadership Without Easy Answers.* Cambridge, Mass.: Harvard University Press, 1995.

Johnson, D. W., Johnson, R. T., and Smith, K. A. *Cooperative Learning: Increasing College Faculty Instructional Productivity.* (2nd ed.) ASHE-ERIC Higher Education Reports No. 4. The George Washington University School of Education and Human Development, 1991.

Keating, P. J., and others. "Change as a Constant: Organizational Restructuring at Carnegie Mellon University." *Business Officer,* 1996, *29*(11), 50–56.

Kezar, A. "Still Trees Without Fruit: Higher Education Research at the Millennium." In *The Review of Higher Education,* forthcoming, Summer 2000.

Rudolph, J. T., and Howard, N. L. "Implementing Total Quality Management at Oregon State University: Moving Continuous Quality Improvement Practices into Higher Education." *CUPA Journal,* 1996, *46*(4), 25–31.

Schein, E. H. "How Can Organizations Learn Faster? The Challenge of Entering the Green Room." *Sloan Management Review,* 1993, *34*(2), 85–92.

PETER ECKEL *is project director, Kellogg Projects on Institutional Transformation, at the American Council on Education.*

ADRIANNA KEZAR *is director of the ERIC Clearinghouse on Higher Education at the George Washington University.*

DEVORAH LIEBERMAN *is vice provost and assistant to the president for campus initiatives and director of teaching and learning at Portland State University.*

8

This chapter examines an organization that for over a decade has offered programs that enable practitioners to become more reflective about their practice and to conduct research that is rooted in practice. They acquire the skills to deal more effectively with the changing higher education landscape. The promise and purposes of think tanks such as these are discussed.

Practitioners as Researchers: Bridging Theory and Practice

Deborah Hirsch

The gap between research and practice is well documented. Higher education researchers and practitioners live in different worlds; they rarely attend the same conferences, write for or read the same journals, and typically have little to say to one another. Theories generated by researchers are developed under conditions that are far removed from the changing, dynamic circumstances of the practitioners' world. Researchers tend to write for one another and for graduate students who pull apart problems and examine them closely under controlled conditions. Administrators rarely read the research literature because they believe it is not written for them.

From the standpoint of administrators, there is little room for research in the turbulent world of practice. The world of administrators has become increasingly fast paced, complex, and situational in an era of unprecedented accountability requirements and rapid change for institutions of higher education. There is little or no time for reflection, theory testing, or knowledge development. Practitioners must think and act on their feet; problems cry for immediate resolution. The consequence is a growing perception that researchers have less and less to say that practitioners find useful or valuable (Schön, 1987, 1995). Hence the *gap*—researchers generate theory, which informs further theory development and refinement; and practitioners draw from their own experience or practical knowledge (Jarvis, 1999).

Most practitioners are so busy responding to demands and crises that they cannot make time to reflect on their practice much less relate it to the theory. With this in mind, the New England Resource Center for Higher Education (NERCHE), founded in 1988, has developed programs to help higher education administrators become more thoughtful about their practice and to conduct research that is rooted in practice. Researchers at the center have collaborated with practitioners both to conduct research and to use the results to help them understand the changing nature of their professions and organizations and to develop the skills to deal with the changes. In addition, NERCHE's *think tanks* for practitioners at the front lines of higher education provide a venue for reflection, interpretation, and analysis. These mechanisms allow practitioners and researchers to engage their work differently.

Currently, NERCHE operates six ongoing think tanks—for chief student affairs officers, chief academic officers, associate academic deans, chief financial officers, department chairs, and heads of institutional research. (See the list at the end of this chapter.) NERCHE has also organized think tanks around its research projects: a project on general education yielded a think tank for faculty and administrators involved in general education programs on their campuses. The Faculty Professional Service Project spun off a think tank for chief academic officers looking to increase support for this activity on their campuses and a think tank for faculty innovators who apply their scholarship to community problems.

Think tanks draw members from the diversity of colleges and universities in New England and meet for intensive daylong seminars on topics ranging from broad issues facing institutions of higher education to particular campus issues and concerns. Over the years, think tanks have involved nearly one thousand individuals from two-thirds of the colleges and universities in the region. Members of the think tanks are selected for their ability as leaders and change agents within their own institutions. Think tank participants interact with counterparts in institutions both similar to and very different from their own. They learn to think beyond their institutional circumstances about issues that influence the industry of higher education researchers and policymakers. They take their knowledge back with them to inform colleagues within their own institutions as well as those whom they have never met.

The think tanks offer one way to bridge the gap between theory and practice. This is accomplished on a variety of levels. First, the think tanks provide a place and space for reflection on practice—*active reflection* (Schön, 1983, 1987, 1995). Think tank curriculum and readings acquaint participants with research and writings that can inform their practice. In addition, think tanks generate research questions that are explored with NERCHE staff, research associates, and think tank members and that lead to participatory research.

Active Reflection

Think tank members—operating at the front lines of higher education—are encouraged both to test their experiential knowledge against theory and to generate their own theory grounded in practice. Schön describes the special knowledge of the practitioner—a knowledge based in action, "When we go about the spontaneous, intuitive performance of the actions of everyday life, we show ourselves to be knowledgeable in a special way. Often we cannot say what we know. . . . Our knowing is ordinarily tacit, implicit in our patterns of action and in our feel for the stuff with which we are dealing. It seems right to say that our knowledge is *in* our action. And similarly, the workaday life of the professional practitioners reveals, in its recognitions, judgments, and skills, a pattern of tacit knowing-in-action" (1995, p. 29).

Practitioners build a body of knowledge about their practice by learning, doing, thinking, and reflecting (Jarvis, 1999). The problem is that as this *knowing-in-practice* becomes increasingly tacit and spontaneous, the practitioner may miss important opportunities to think about what he or she is doing, hence the importance of reflection, which allows the practitioner to surface and critique the tacit understandings associated with repetitive experiences. As reflective researchers of their own practice, practitioners can generate new knowledge, thereby recasting the relationship between research and practice. "There is no question of an 'exchange' between research and practice or of the 'implementation' of research results" (Schön, 1983, pp. 308–309).

Unfortunately, there is little time or encouragement for most higher education administrators to reflect on their practice on their own. Therefore one of the most valuable functions of the think tanks is to create a safe time and space for participants to leave the ever pressing demands of their jobs to come together to reflect on their experience. The meetings are planned to stimulate serious reflection by members on their own practice. This is done using a variety of techniques, including trigger cases, role plays, and provocative questions that encourage members to think outside their own experience to bring in broader institutional and theoretical perspectives. Our experience indicates that participants know a lot that they do not realize they know, and in the process of meeting and talking as a group they are able to draw out what they know in conversation with their peers. "Reflection-in-action occurs in the medium of words. It makes explicit the action strategies, assumptions, models of the world, or problem-settings that were implicit" (Schön, 1995, pp. 30–31). After each discussion, NERCHE staff help participants analyze and reflect on what they know, present models or theories from relevant research, and note any themes, patterns, and inconsistencies. The structure of the think tanks includes a curriculum of readings drawn from relevant literature to ground discussions in theory and research. Readings are sent out in advance of the meetings to inform discussions, which weave back and forth between theory and reflection on practice. Participants are encouraged to analyze, interpret, and apply what they read to their own practice as well as to the experiences of colleagues from a diverse group of institutions. The think tanks are designed to help members credit what they know as real knowledge and to push them through structured inquiry to generate and test new knowledge for action. This "reflection on knowing—and reflection-in-action can give rise to actionable theory" (Schön, 1995, p. 31).

This process of generating and testing new knowledge for action is embedded in theories of *action research*. The problem is that the academy does not place equal value on action research, compared with the research of discovery, as a legitimate way to generate knowledge. However, this may be changing, as evidenced in the widespread interest in Boyer's landmark publication *Scholarship Reconsidered* (1990), which challenges the prevailing epistemology underlying scholarship in the academy to include the scholarship of integration, of application, and of teaching, in addition to the scholarship of discovery or basic research. Through practice, these forms of scholarship can, according to Boyer and followers, conform to the same academic standards and rigor as the more traditional scholarship of discovery that is typically associated with research.

Participatory Action Research

Another way to recast the relationship between researchers and practitioners is to involve practitioners in the research process itself. "Participatory research attempts to break down the distinction between the researchers and the researched, the subjects and objects of knowledge, production by the participation of the people-for-themselves in the process of gaining and creating knowledge" (Park, Brydon-Miller, Hall, and Jackson, 1993, p. 34). Participatory or action research involves those in the "real world" in determining the questions, collecting the data, and analyzing the results in order to solve problems and bring about change. Action research has particular resonance for practitioners seeking to bring about change and to solidify commitment to change. There are some distinct advantages to using this methodology for these purposes. It lends credibility by providing information and understanding to a broad audience. It helps identify points in the system that can be challenged by action. It increases participants' understanding of themselves and their problems and raises commitment to change. It can serve as an organizing strategy to get people involved and active around a particular issue. And it develops confidence in the ability to take action based on hard data rather than on feeling (Bogdan and Biklen, 1982). "The result of this kind of activity is living knowledge that gets translated directly into action, because it is created with this concrete appropriation in mind" (Park, Brydon-Miller, Hall, and Jackson, p. 3). Unlike traditional research in which theory, developed by the researchers or academics, is used to illuminate practice, participatory action research invites the practitioners to develop context-rich theories of their practice and then use these theories to effect change.

NERCHE's use of think tanks as a mechanism to help administrators reflect on practice has given rise to a number of participatory action research projects. The design of these research and action projects is guided by the basic principles behind participatory research methodology. This research method seeks to be a direct and immediate benefit to the community, involves the community in the research process, increases community awareness and commitment, is viewed as a dialogue over time, and fosters mobilization of resources for the solution of problems (Hall, 1977).

A recent example is NERCHE's effort to work with a group of ten institutions that are undertaking significant change in order to strengthen civic learning among undergraduates. In a learning network or cluster, not unlike a NERCHE think tank, researchers and practitioners will develop theories about educational transformation (widespread change) through reflection on their change process. In addition, participating institutions will create a base for change among other institutions. This project is intentional about including a team of key stakeholders from each institution as co-investigators in the change process. In this way, theory is developed not only to advance the knowledge of the researchers but also to enrich the learning opportunities for the practitioners, which is necessary for creating a political and advocacy base for change. Regular communication among participants and researchers, including conference calls, Web and e-mail interactions, site visits, and several face-to-face meetings, will create opportunities to process experiences, develop hypotheses, and test and refine theories over the life of the project. "If there is any one methodological feature that distinguishes participatory research, . . . it is dialogue. . . . As a tool of research, dialogue produces not just factual knowledge but also interpersonal and critical knowledge . . . so they may know themselves better as individuals and as a community" (Park, Brydon-Miller, Hall, and Jackson, pp. 12–13).

This model is deliberately different from traditional models in which outside researchers conduct the research, present at conferences, and publish journal articles and books that have limited general impact on institutions of higher education. Instead this project is designed deliberately to develop leadership within the cluster institutions in order to promote change on their campuses and to stimulate change on other campuses. To support this end, dissemination will occur in a variety of forms throughout the life of the cluster, rather than as a single, final product. Frequent contacts with pertinent projects and national associations will be initiated and maintained. Cluster members will collaborate in conducting interactive workshops at national and regional conferences and will consult with interested institutions. Case studies and other materials based on the work of the cluster will be used in workshops, which will emphasize interactive problem solving, action planning, and organizational analysis. Publications in research-oriented journals and practitioner trade journals will contribute to a body of knowledge about institutional change and about civic engagement aimed at a wide-ranging audience.

Conclusion

There are a number of strategies and mechanisms for bridging the gap between research and practice that have been described in this volume. There is a large body of knowledge about action research, participant action research, and community-based research that can inform the subject.

Recently, a number of authors (Schön 1983, 1987; Jarvis, 1999) have questioned the high status conferred on theory that is generated by researchers who are disconnected from the fluid and dynamic experience of those in the field. These writers suggest that the gap might be a result of viewing practitioners as the locus for applying or testing theory. However, the problems of practitioners tend not to lend themselves to being solved by empirically based knowledge. These issues are complex, multidimensional, and conflicting. Instead the gap might be diminished if practitioners are given the tools and opportunities to generate theory that is steeped in the messiness of the field, wherein lie the "problems of greatest human concern" (Schön, 1987, p. 3).

Therefore instead of thinking about how we can make better use of researcher-based knowledge, perhaps we should be thinking about what we can learn from practitioners. As practitioners become reflective researchers, the gap dissipates. The NERCHE think tanks have proved to be successful at creating a place and a space for practitioners in higher education to reflect on their own practice, compare their experiences with colleagues, and connect to theory as well as develop their own grounded theories as they work to address both local and regional issues. Though most of the think tank members have been faculty and scholars in their own disciplines, their administrative roles have made reflection and scholarship difficult, if not impossible. The think tank, composed of people at the vanguard of higher education, provides an opportunity to read, think, and talk about larger issues with colleagues. It also provides an opportunity to generate ideas about problems that need to be researched and creates opportunities to carry out the research.

The process of developing and working with the think tanks has extended and informed NERCHE's research agenda, which uses a collaborative participatory action research model to develop the questions to be studied, the methodology to be employed, the dissemination of results, and the implementation of change. For over a decade, NERCHE has focused on encouraging reflection, stimulating collaborative thinking and action, and generating research and action projects aimed at the most pressing issues that shape and reshape the modern academic community. NERCHE has been able to sustain and nurture this model, in part, because of its status as a center within the university. Centers such as this serve as *enclaves* that provide protected environments for innovation, support for alternative modes of scholarship, such as applied research, and opportunities to broaden the scope of their projects through collaboration (Singleton, Hirsch, and Burack, 1999). Researchers in traditional tenure track faculty lines have little incentive to break out of traditional research models to employ user-friendly methodologies and certainly have almost no protection if they choose to do so. Until this kind of scholarly activity is seen as legitimate, the gap between researchers and practitioners will remain wide and unfathomable. "Introducing the new scholarship means becoming involved in an epistemological battle. It is a battle of snails, proceeding so slowly that you have to look very carefully in order to see it going on. But it is happening nonetheless" (Schön, 1995, p. 32).

New England Resource Center for Higher Education Think Tanks

The following is a brief description of each of NERCHE's think tanks.

Chief Student Affairs Officers Think Tank is composed of leading student affairs administrators in the region. The two themes of community and diversity have featured strongly in discussions since the group was founded in 1988. The sessions consider major issues and changes in higher education in terms of the impact on student life and learning; for example, restructuring, the use of technology, violence on campus, and assessment. Members have identified effective strategies for leadership; developed workshops, presentations, and publications; and consulted widely on one another's campuses.

Chief Academic Officers Think Tank discusses a variety of higher education issues, always focusing squarely on the policy implications of the members' work. In the past three years, the group has spent much of its time examining faculty roles and rewards. In addition, the group has addressed fundamental questions about the future of the U.S. system of higher education, the issue of accreditation and accountability, and the civic role for institutions of higher education.

Associate Academic Deans Think Tank includes individuals with responsibilities spanning academic advising, faculty support, and curriculum development. Members share an intense commitment to ensuring that students' academic experiences are supportive and rich. The group has discussed a range of topics in this realm, which include academic integrity, articulation and transfer, student retention, developmental education, and incorporating diversity and multiculturalism in the curriculum. Members of the group convened a special session with student affairs counterparts on helping faculty respond to the needs of both disabled and disturbed students.

Chief Financial Officers Think Tank consists of members who think far beyond the bottom line. The group has considered the critical issues facing higher education and the role they play in working collaboratively with faculty and other members of the administration to institute changes that will improve the environment for learning and enhance productivity.

Department Chairs Think Tank provides ongoing support, mentoring, and skill development for members. Topics have followed issues that have received national attention, such as team building and collective responsibility, ways of creating multidimensional incentives and rewards for faculty, and assessment and uses of technology to promote student learning. Members are in the process of preparing workshops and materials to share with their colleagues to enhance the ability of chairs to become leaders and change agents.

Institutional Researchers Think Tank offers a forum for leaders of these key units to explore the demanding, complex, and shifting roles that they play in institutions driven by demands for accountability and assessment. These individuals must balance the needs and demands of their own institutions with a range of external constituents, including state and federal officials, trustees, leaders in the business community, and media organizations. In doing so, they must address a broad and changing array of issues in higher education. They play a pivotal role in influencing both policy and research agendas.

References

Bogdan, R. C., and Biklen, S. K. *Qualitative Research for Education*. Needham Heights, Mass.: Allyn & Bacon, 1982.

Boyer, E. L. *Scholarship Reconsidered: Priorities of the Professoriate*. Princeton, N.J.: Carnegie Foundation for the Advancement of Teaching, 1990.

Hall, B. *Creating Knowledge: Breaking the Monopoly*. Toronto: Participatory Research Project of the International Council for Adult Education, 1977.

Jarvis, P. *The Practitioner-Researcher: Developing Theory from Practice*. San Francisco: Jossey-Bass, 1999.

Park, P., Brydon-Miller, M., Hall, B., and Jackson, T. *Voices of Change: Participatory Research in the United States and Canada*. New York: Bergin & Garvey, 1993.

Schön, D. A. *The Reflective Practitioner: How Professionals Think in Action*. New York: Basic Books, 1983.

Schön, D. A. *Educating the Reflective Practitioner*. San Francisco: Jossey-Bass, 1987.

Schön, D. A. "The New Scholarship Requires a New Epistemology: Knowing-in-Action." *Change*, 1995, 27(6), 26–39.

Singleton, S., Hirsch, D., and Burack, C. "Organizational Structures for Community Engagement." In P. G. Bringle, P. Games, and E. A. Malloy (eds.), *Colleges and Universities as Citizens*. Needham, Mass.: Allyn & Bacon, 1999.

Deborah Hirsch is director of the New England Resource Center for Higher Education at the University of Massachusetts-Boston.

9

*National organizations such as associations can be
change agents working at a system level to assist in
building bridges between researchers and practitioners
to close the research-to-practice gap. This requires
associations to become more familiar with researchers
and to use their annual conferences and publications to
make practitioners aware of the importance of research
to inform their practice.*

Bridging the Gap:
Multiple Players,
Multiple Approaches

Madeleine F. Green

Higher education is full of paradoxes, and the topic of this volume is a rich
illustration. How is it that the academy holds research in such high value
but devalues or ignores research about itself? And why should the field of
education, a topic of staggering national and international importance,
occupy so low a status in the hierarchy of academic fields? No less contradictory, as Colbeck points out in Chapter Three, is the fact that many
researchers in higher education were once practitioners themselves, yet
their research is either not designed to be useful to practitioners or is not
perceived as such. And finally, there is the paradox that higher education
programs rarely play a role of resource to their own institutions. Institutional decision makers may be more interested in generating data that serve
public relations purposes than in generating formative evaluation. On the
other side of the equation, as Peterson points out in Chapter Two,
researchers fear being derailed from their academic agendas by getting
drawn into the business of the institution.

The Great Divide

The practice-research divide is one of many contradictory behavior patterns
found in colleges and universities. In the eyes of most stakeholders, the low
status of teaching in an enterprise whose major function is teaching is
another conspicuous paradox that in the last decade has received much
deserved national attention. Even in teaching institutions, the drive for status

often shifts the balance of prestige and faculty rewards toward research. Most doctoral programs pay no attention at all to preparing their graduates to teach; young faculty are largely on their own to learn the craft. The national project Preparing Future Faculty sponsored by the American Association of Colleges and Universities and the Council of Graduate Schools has made an important contribution to addressing this issue through partnerships between doctoral programs and teaching institutions. But there is a great deal to be done in this arena.

Similarly, academic administrators are to a large extent amateur managers, highly trained in their disciplines but ill prepared for their administrative and leadership tasks. As educational institutions, colleges and universities pay surprisingly little attention to the ongoing development of their faculty and staff. Surely, no business would ignore its most important (and expensive) asset, and indeed the large corporate budgets devoted to training and development demonstrate that many corporations do a lot more than pay lip service to human resource development. The paucity of resources devoted to faculty and staff development in higher education speaks volumes.

That higher education is growing more aware of these contradictions is surely a good thing. The complexity of higher education institutions as organizations and the fierce pressures for accountability and for responsiveness to their many stakeholders make it imperative that colleges and universities recognize and take advantage of the many resources and opportunities available to them. And surely, knowledge about higher education itself is one of those resources. But even if there is an emerging recognition that the gap between research and practice is dysfunctional, finding solutions is another matter.

Solutions for Crossing the Divide

The contributors to this volume have described the gap between research and practice, analyzed its probable causes, and offered various solutions. The strategies proposed are not surprisingly directed mostly to the affected parties—individual researchers and practitioners.

Although changing faculty attitudes and behaviors is no small undertaking, several authors see this as central. Cross (Chapter Five) suggests that researchers must take responsibility for the impact of their research on practice, just as teachers must be held accountable for their students' learning. As a precondition for this to occur, researchers must acknowledge that the role of research is to produce improvement in practice. Even if the research is relevant to practice and of high quality, there is no guarantee that it will be disseminated in user-friendly form, so that it is useful to busy practitioners. Therefore strategic dissemination and good presentation are key. Kezar's study (discussed in Chapter One) underscores this point, emphasizing that practitioners want above all short, provocative, and well-written pieces. Frequently cited examples of such useful pieces are Boyer's *Scholarship Reconsidered* (1990) and Chickering and Gamson's *Applying the Seven Principles for Good Practice in Undergraduate Education* (1991). Meeting this expectation would require a considerable change in the focus and style of most higher education researchers.

Colbeck also focuses on the behavior of faculty members, urging young faculty to take the risk of making their research more relevant to practice. She correctly urges senior faculty, who establish the criteria for promotion and tenure, to change the reward system and the culture, so that useful research is rewarded rather than denigrated as insufficiently academic. Without such change, it will be unlikely for junior faculty to take such risks.

A second set of suggested solutions offered by the authors are addressed to practitioners. Practitioners rarely read the higher education journals. Many are downright proud of their ignorance of the higher education literature and of their preparation for the managerial tasks that consume their professional lives. Changing their mind-sets and their approach to their work is an important piece of the equation in bringing together theory and practice.

To encourage administrators to be more reflective about their work, the New England Resource Center on Higher Education (NERCHE) convenes groups of administrators in New England in think tanks to engage as researchers of their own practice and develop their theory from the ground up. This approach engages primarily practitioners; outside experts beyond NERCHE staff are rarely invited, based on the assumption that "sufficient knowledge resides in the group" and that readings and discussion are the keys to building theory. In Chapter Six, Ramaley suggests that academic leadership should be viewed as a scholarly act, turning the institution into a living laboratory characterized by constant inquiry, testing of ideas, and seeking out the data that can help guide leaders who live in the murky swamp of ill-defined problems and elusive solutions. The development of an institutional studies office, staffed by higher education researchers, would provide a mechanism to ground the discussion and the decision-making process of academic leaders in the literature that could be applied to practice. Eckel, Kezar, and Lieberman (Chapter Seven) present a variation of this idea, citing reading groups as a useful way to turn the scholarly attention of faculty and administrators to institutional issues. In Chapter Four, Conrad and Gunter take the idea even further, suggesting that campuses establish learning communities consisting of researchers and administrators who meet regularly to identify which issues need to be studied, what research is available, and what else needs to be done. These ideas pick up on an important theme of this volume: neither group *telling* the other what it wants or needs or serving as a *subject* for the other will bring about a satisfactory conclusion.

Working at the institutional level, as Ramaley; Eckel, Kezar, and Lieberman; and Cross suggest is certainly an important way to help bridge the gap. But in addition to effecting institutional changes that occur one institution at a time, are there ways to influence how the higher education community as a whole addresses the research-practice issue? Enter the foundations and national higher education associations.

As is the case for many issues of reform in higher education, change usually occurs institution by institution but in the context of national awareness and debate. External pressure inevitably accelerates the process. Assessment and the push for institutions to become more learning centered are just two examples of national (and international) movements that have produced considerable change on college and university campuses. But creating a movement is no small undertaking. Foundations, by their choice of where they direct funding, and national associations, by their choice of the issues they emphasize (which in turn receive foundation funding), can play an important role in launching national discussion and providing legitimacy for new ways of thinking and doing business.

The Role of Associations and Funders

So what might be the role of associations and funders (foundations and government) in the meaningful reexamination of higher education research and practice? Let us begin with the higher education associations. A large number of their membership are administrators; hence the associations have access to the presidents, chief academic officers, and deans who are the potential reflective practitioners. The capacity to draw attention to an issue and the ability to disseminate information are perhaps the strongest suits of national associations. The lament of practitioners that the research is neither readily available in user-friendly form nor addressed to the needs of practitioners suggests that higher education associations could render a real service by performing these functions. *In short, the associations have the capacity to serve as translators and disseminators of useful research, putting it in a format that meets the needs of busy practitioners.*

Another historical strength of associations is the convening function. As Hirsch (Chapter Eight) points out in describing NERCHE's think tanks, bringing together presidents, chief academic officers, or deans to learn from one another in a space dedicated to reflection is a useful service. Such forums must be carefully planned, however, for there is always the potential of these sessions serving more as therapy for beleaguered administrators (not a trivial outcome) than as means to improve practice. National meetings and leadership development programs present an important opportunity to ground the discussion in research and to push the discussion deeper than the level of superficial good practice. In short, we in the associations would do well to consistently model the behavior of grounding our own work in the relevant research.

The American Association of Higher Education (AAHE) provides an exemplar of how a national association can create a sustained dialogue that involves theory and practice. AAHE has kept the issue of student learning, as well as the related topics of faculty roles and rewards and assessment, high on its agenda for close to a decade. The scholarship of teaching and learning forms the basis for large gatherings of faculty and for publications of good practice and resource materials. AAHE has successfully engaged large numbers in a serious examination of teaching and learning, creating a sizable cohort of reflective practitioners.

Another aspect of convening would be to provide a forum for researchers, policymakers, and practitioners to discuss these issues. As a first step, the American Council on Education (ACE) convened a small group of foundation, institution, and association leaders to identify their perceptions of the gap between research, practice, and policymaking. As a result of this initial conversation, ACE plans to initiate a broader dialogue of associations, foundations, researchers, and campus leaders to suggest ways to address this issue at a national level. This is an ambitious undertaking, and the payoffs could be considerable.

·A more focused attempt to bring the relevant players to the table is the Kellogg Forum on Higher Education Transformation, a partnership of colleges and universities, organizations, and research centers whose purpose is to learn together about transforming higher education, so that it can become more flexible, accountable, collaborative, and responsive. The colleges and universities are Alverno College, the University of Arizona, Portland State University, and the Minnesota State College and University System. The organizations and resource centers include the American Council on Education, the Higher Education Research Institute at the University of California-Los Angeles, the Center for Higher and Postsecondary Education at the University of Michigan, and the New England Resource Center for Higher Education at the University of Massachusetts-Boston. The forum was created by the W. K. Kellogg Foundation and is an ambitious experiment in collaboration. This group aims to combine the learning from research and practice in ways that will yield new insights into institutional change. A further goal is to take its learning beyond the partnership itself and—based on the knowledge it creates—engage the wider higher education community in a dialogue about transformation. How this will be done is still being worked out, but these are the important strategies that associations and institutions need to be working together to shape.

A final role of the associations is to stimulate research on issues of national importance and engage the researchers in their deliberations, policymaking, and forums. In pursuing its long-standing agenda on diversity, ACE convenes the researchers on this topic, identifying gaps in the research to stimulate further work and connecting researchers who are working on this topic. One important way to stimulate research is with funding, but even in the absence of sure sources, the identification of important topics can have positive results.

These approaches do not prevent associations from conducting research by themselves or in partnership with researchers. Many of the associations have staff capacity, which can be considerably enhanced by teaming up with academic researchers. Associations can work collaboratively in the actual conduct of the research, engage academics as advisers to the process, or commission research.

In short, the associations representing administrators and institutions can make a real contribution to bridging the gap by convening, disseminating, collaborating, commissioning, and stimulating research. And as Ramaley suggests for campus leaders, the associations would do well themselves to take the research seriously, approaching their own agendas in a scholarly way. Although the higher education associations are not scholarly organizations, there is no reason for us not to apply the principles of good scholarship in our approach to issues.

Another important group of associations that can influence dialogue and behavior from a national perch are the associations of higher education faculty members and researchers. The publications and conferences of the Association for the Study of Higher Education, Division J of the American Educational Research Association, and the Association for Institutional Research do not attract practitioners, perhaps, as Peterson suggests, because of the drive for professionalization of the field. As Peterson notes, higher education, like other fields, is not immune to the paradigm wars; and administrators have abundant and more urgent battles to fight. Because they set the agenda for the field, disciplinary associations have the greatest potential to influence faculty. These associations have the capacity to shift the focus of higher education faculty toward research that is directly relevant to practitioners. Such a change of focus would require debate about research paradigms, greater discussion of the link between research and practice, and as Colbeck notes, a shift in the editorial policies of the journals.

A final and crucial actor is funders. Peterson points out the paucity of funding currently available to higher education researchers. Those foundations that do fund higher education (and some have shifted their interest to K–12) devote little, if any, of their funds to research. Needless to say, the foundations could play a major role in stimulating research in general and particularly in sponsoring research targeted to improving practice. Perhaps the associations need to build in money for research on projects that are funded. Perhaps institutions also need to think about including assessment of projects as part of their grant submission. The federal government also provides very modest amounts of funds to campus researchers through some open grants competition and through its centers for research and development. Herein lies yet another paradox: if education reform is indeed a priority for foundations and government, why is there so little support for research that could improve practice?

Final Thoughts

The old saw about politicians who do not want to be confused by the facts surely should not apply to higher education. But we seem to be stuck in a bind for which all parties bear responsibilities. Just as higher education professors and researchers need to take collective responsibility for the direction of their field, so do institutional leaders, who are in the best position to change the institutional culture of deliberation and decision making. Beyond the institutional level, associations can exert a powerful impact on shaping the dialogue, serving as translator and disseminator, and "walking the walk" that demonstrates we do value the facts. Finally, funders, both the government and foundations, set the agenda in important ways through their decisions about how they focus their resources and what results they expect. Like any significant change, this one will require multiple actors and sustained attention.

References

Boyer, E. L. *Scholarship Reconsidered: Priorities of the Professoriate.* Princeton, N.J.: Carnegie Foundation for the Advancement of Teaching, 1990.

Chickering, A. W., and Gamson, Z. F. (eds.). *Applying the Seven Principles for Good Practice in Undergraduate Education.* New Directions for Teaching and Learning, no. 47. San Francisco: Jossey-Bass, 1991.

MADELEINE F. GREEN is vice president and director of the Center for Institutional and International Initiatives of the American Council on Education.

INDEX

Back Issue/Subscription Order Form

Copy or detach and send to:
Jossey-Bass Inc., 350 Sansome Street, San Francisco CA 94104-1342

Call or fax toll free!
Phone 888-378-2537 6AM–5PM PST; Fax 800-605-2665

Back issues: Please send me the following issues at $23 each.
(Important: please include series initials and issue number, such as HE90.)

1. HE _____

_____

_____

$ _____ Total for single issues

$ _____ Shipping charges (for single issues *only;* subscriptions are exempt from shipping charges): Up to $30, add $5^{50} • $30^{01}–$50, add $6^{50} $50^{01}–$75, add $8 • $75^{01}–$100, add $10 • $100^{01}–$150, add $12 Over $150, call for shipping charge.

Subscriptions   Please ❏ start   ❏ renew my subscription to *New Directions for Higher Education* for the year _____ at the following rate:

U.S.	❏ Individual $58	❏ Institutional $104
Canada:	❏ Individual $83	❏ Institutional $129
All Others:	❏ Individual $88	❏ Institutional $134

NOTE: Subscriptions are quarterly, and are for the calendar year only. Subscriptions begin with the Spring issue of the year indicated above.

$ _____ Total single issues and subscriptions (Add appropriate sales tax for your state for single issue orders. No sales tax on U.S. subscriptions. Canadian residents, add GST for subscriptions and single issues.)

❏ Payment enclosed (U.S. check or money order only)
❏ VISA, MC, AmEx, Discover Card # _____ Exp. date_____

Signature _____ Day phone _____
❏ Bill me (U.S. institutional orders only. Purchase order required.)
Purchase order #_____
Federal Tax ID 135593032   GST 89102-8052

Name _____
Address _____

_____

Phone_____ E-mail _____

For more information about Jossey-Bass, visit our Web site at:
www.josseybass.com   **PRIORITY CODE = ND1**